Preach the Word!

A Collection of Essays on Biblical Preaching in Honor of Jerry Vines

David L. Allen
General Editor

Peter Lumpkins
Managing Editor

Preach the Word!
A Collection of Essays on Biblical Preaching in Honor of Jerry Vines
David L. Allen, General Editor
Peter Lumpkins, Managing Editor

Copyright 2013 © Free Church Press

Unless otherwise indicated, Scripture verses are from The King James Version of the Holy Bible

Scripture quotations marked (ESV) are from The Holy Bible, English Standard Version® (ESV®), copyright © 2001 by Crossway, a publishing ministry of Good News Publishers. Used by permission. All rights reserved.

Scripture quotations taken from the New American Standard Bible®, Copyright © 1960, 1962, 1963, 1968, 1971, 1972, 1973, 1975, 1977, 1995 by The Lockman Foundation Used by permission. Lockman.org

Scripture quotations marked (NIV) are taken from the Holy Bible, New International Version®, NIV®. Copyright © 1973, 1978, 1984, 2011 by Biblica, Inc.™ Used by permission of Zondervan. All rights reserved worldwide. www.zondervan.com The "NIV" and "New International Version" are trademarks registered in the United States Patent and Trademark Office by Biblica, Inc.™

Scripture quotations marked HCSB are taken from the Holman Christian Standard Bible®, Copyright © 1999, 2000, 2002, 2003 by Holman Bible Publishers. Used by permission. Holman Christian Standard Bible®, Holman CSB®, and HCSB® are federally registered trademarks of Holman Bible Publishers.

Scripture taken from the New King James Version®. Copyright © 1982 by Thomas Nelson, Inc. Used by permission. All rights reserved.

Revised Standard Version of the Bible, copyright 1952 [2nd edition, 1971] by the Division of Christian Education of the National Council of the Churches of Christ in the United States of America. Used by permission. All rights reserved.

Printed in the United States.

Jacket design—Jessica Anglea, www.jessicaanglea.com

Interior design—Debbie Patrick, Vision Run www.visionrun.com

ISBN: 978-1-939283-01-6

Free Church Press
P. O. Box Box 1075
Carrollton, GA 30112

Contents

Dedication Page
A Reader's Note by Peter Lumpkins, Managing Editor 7
Foreword by David L. Allen, General Editor 11

Part I: The Preacher

A Brief Look into the Life of the Preacher: Jerry Vines
by Emir and Ergun Caner 17

A Personal Testimony to the Power of Biblical Preaching
by Johnny Hunt 29

Simple Biblicism:
The Word of God in the Theology of Jerry Vines
by Malcolm B. Yarnell III 37

Part II: The Preached Word

The Preaching Event: A True Baptist Distinctive
by O.S. Hawkins 53

The Church's Necessity for 21st Century Survival
by Steven Smith 67

Preaching the Whole Counsel of God
by Paige Patterson 77

Measuring Success in Biblical Preaching
by Stephen Rummage 91

A Theology of Expository Preaching
by Steve Lemke 101

Part III: The Preacher as Pastor

The Importance of Biblical Preaching
in Building a Great Church
by Adam B. Dooley 119

Biblical Preaching in a Mega-Church Setting
by Mac Brunson 131

Part IV: The Preacher as Evangelist

Do the Work of an Evangelist
by Jeff Pennington 141

Growing a Church through Evangelistic, Biblical Preaching
by Steve Gaines 155

Part V: The Preacher Preaching

A Word from the Late Dr. Adrian Rogers
on the Preaching of Jerry Vines *173*

A Baptist and His Bible:
A Biblical Sermon Based on 2 Timothy 3:14–4:13
by Jerry Vines 175

End Notes..193
List of Contributors 209
About Dr. Jerry Vines 211

Dedication

*W*e gratefully dedicate this collection of essays on Biblical preaching in honor of Jerry Vines to two extraordinary churches which Dr. Vines served as Pastor for almost thirty years combined, faithfully preaching and teaching God's Holy Word. Therefore,

*T*o the First Baptist Church, Jacksonville, Florida and her present Senior Pastor, Dr. Mac Brunson, we enthusiastically dedicate this collection of essays on Biblical preaching published in honor of your former pastor, Dr. Jerry Vines. As he stood for years and proclaimed with prophetic boldness "Thus saith the Lord," you listened to him excitedly, learned with him respectfully, remained loyal to him willingly, and loved him genuinely such that, in the end, he could, with the Apostle Paul, say "Yea, so have I strived to preach the gospel ..." (Romans 15:20). And, furthermore, your faithful prayers and material support in making this publication possible reflect the relationship the New Testament exhorts between shepherd and flock.

*T*o the Dauphin Way Baptist Church, Mobile, Alabama, and her present Senior Pastor, Dr. Adam B. Dooley, we enthusiastically dedicate this collection of essays on Biblical preaching published in honor of your former pastor, Dr. Jerry Vines. For years, you warmly encouraged him, graciously loved him, humbly listened to him, and excitedly watched as God used him to build up the Body of Christ by being instant in season and out; reproving, rebuking, and exhorting with all longsuffering and doctrine as he obeyed the Apostolic call to "Preach the word" (2 Timothy 4:2). And, furthermore, your faithful prayers and material support in making this publication possible reflect the relationship the New Testament exhorts between shepherd and flock.

I charge thee therefore before God, and the Lord Jesus Christ, who shall judge the quick and the dead at his appearing and his kingdom; Preach the word; be instant in season, out of season; reprove, rebuke, exhort with all longsuffering and doctrine."

The Apostle Paul
(2 Timothy 4:1-2)

A Collection of Essays on Biblical Preaching in Honor of Jerry Vines

A Reader's Note from the Managing Editor

Frequently in the academic world a respected professor is honored by several of his close colleagues or former students (or a combination of both) for the massive impact he or she has undeniably produced within a particular discipline during his or her lifetime academic career. The official term for the collection of essays is *Festschrift*, a term borrowed from the German language, literally meaning "festival writing." The intended result, therefore, is a celebratory piece of literature wherein several authors each devote a chapter commending the lifework of the one to whom the *Festschrift* is dedicated. More often than not, each contributor will have been *personally* impacted by the professor's influence. It is in the spirit of *Festschrift* that this present collection of essays is dedicated to Dr. Jerry Vines.

As the reader will note from the list of impressive contributors to this volume, Dr. Vines' influence as an expositor of God's Word remains both broad and deep. Few men over the past fifty years have had the reach he has had in influencing those who "Preach the Word." Undoubtedly, history will continue to cite Dr. Vines as one of the brightest pulpit lights within his denomination, The Southern Baptist Convention. Indeed, Vines' sermon *A Baptist and His Bible*, first preached at the 1987 Pastors' Conference in St. Louis, Missouri, has been judged, in part, as one of the solidifying events which recaptured the convention for conservative Southern Baptists. Evidence of Jerry Vines' influence as a pulpiteer during the years of the "Conservative Resurgence" is illustrated in the documentary book entitled *In the Name of the Father: The Rhetoric of the New Southern Baptist Convention* (Carbondale: Southern Illinois University Press, 1999). Two reputable professors of communication indicated that, "While fifteen years (1979-1994) of SBC convention preaching has provided hours of Scripture-reading and argumentation for the development of the inerrancy case, no preacher has said it better than Jerry Vines" (p.56).

Carl L. Kell and L. Raymond Camp each served as professors of communications at two prestigious universities at the time they penned their 1999 book. The academic researchers described Dr. Vines' 1987 sermon at length and offered their studied estimation not only of the sermonic impact of the message itself, but also their academic evaluation of Dr. Vines as a successful communicator and Biblical expositor. In short, they judged Vines as altogether representing what they indicated as, "a high rhetorical watermark in Southern Baptist preaching." They write:

> *Vines' sermon "A Baptist and His Bible" is the finest national statement on Biblical inerrancy we found during our research for this study.* Jerry Vines did not disappoint, as he has always been a gifted speaker and an ardent student of the Bible's native languages— Hebrew and Greek ... In a firm, memorized textual speaking style, Vines riveted the audience to their seats for nearly forty minutes.
>
> ... The power of a literate, prepared text and clear purpose combined with Jerry Vines' folksy rhetorical style, provided a defining moment in raising Southern Baptist preaching to a new level ... *This sermon was a high rhetorical watermark in Southern Baptist preaching.*
>
> (pp.56-57; italics added)

The professors go on to conclude that even though The Southern Baptist Convention had experienced through the years many great preaching events by many capable men, yet when "Vines strode to the plexiglass [sic] pulpit, acknowledged his audience, paused, and then spoke ... *everyone present knew this sermon was special*"(italics added).

Hence, this cluster of essays in book form represents the collective celebratory appreciation indicative not only of the contributors to the volume, but of thousands of Southern Baptists everywhere who have been positively influenced by the Biblical preaching of Jerry Vines.

I want to especially thank Dr. David Allen, Dean, School of Theology and Professor of Preaching at Southwestern Baptist Theological Seminary in Fort Worth, Texas, for graciously serving as General Editor of this volume. Dr. Allen was the obvious choice to editorially lead this project as the reader will easily glean from the editorial *Foreword* he provides. He and Dr. Vines have a deep relationship from which Dr. Allen has surely been fruitfully blessed through the years. Not only so, but Dr. Allen's academic background in both New Testament exegesis and preaching provided the scholarly but practical requirements to complete the volume you now read.

Following Dr. Allen's *Foreword*, a virtual "Who's who" in Southern Baptist life line up one after another not only reflecting the inspiration they received from God's work in Vines' life and ministry, but offering both wise counsel to practice preaching and a solid Biblical-theological framework to understand the non-negotiable significance Biblical preaching possesses for the modern church. Indeed if the New Testament church is to survive in the twenty-first century, then we must practice more Biblical preaching not less.

After the essays, the reader will find the full manuscript of "A Baptist and His Bible," a sermon by Dr. Vines quoted many times over by friend and foe alike. Know we remain well aware that the act of preaching is a unique event in itself involving the necessary intermingling of the personalities involved—proclaimer, recipient, and the Holy Spirit as He moves upon the faithful deliverance of the Word He inspired. Or, as Phillips Brooks, the nineteenth century master pulpit communicator put it, preaching is "communication of truth through personality." Even so, the manuscript carries a particular power all its own, a Divine power about which we may confidently testify each time we glean some of the classic sermons of men who long ago left this world behind to be with the One for Whom they faithfully labored in the Word. Though dead, we find their preaching *lives*.

Before the sermon manuscript, however, we thought it especially fitting to republish words from the late and legendary Dr. Adrian Rogers, past president of the Southern Baptist Convention, Senior Pastor of the Bellevue Baptist Church, Cordova, Tennessee, and an unchallenged statesman and rhetorical architect of the "Conservative Resurgence" of the Southern Baptist Convention. Arguably, Dr. Rogers was the most influential pastor in the Southern Baptist Convention, a position he did not seek but nonetheless held for perhaps the last fifteen years of his life. Note again Kell and Camp's description of the excitement Dr. Rogers exuded as he introduced Vines in 1987:

> Adrian Rogers, president of the SBC in 1987 and regarded as the quintessential orator of Southern Baptist life, introduced Vines. In all of the hours of videotape and transcript involving Adrian

Rogers, he was never so humbled nor excited when referring to others on the podium. Vines was, for Rogers, "the best combination of scholar and country preacher in Southern Baptist life today."

Dr. Rogers' opening words first appeared as a *Foreword* to another edition of "A Baptist and His Bible" published by *Jerry Vines Ministries* (www.jerryvines.com). We are especially grateful to *Love Worth Finding* (www.lwf.org), the ongoing radio and television ministry of the late Dr. Rogers, in giving us full permission to publish Rogers' commendation of "A Baptist and His Bible."

One final word: each essay in this volume is a single unit and purposely designed to stand on its own. We gave much liberty to the contributors in offering their individual skills, expertise, and personal relationship with Dr. Vines toward successfully reaching a common goal of a *celebration* publication. It should be no surprise, then, for occasional overlap to occur. We felt any slight redundancy was irrelevant to successfully meeting our goal for this volume. We hope and expect the reader to agree. And finally, the editors are also aware there can be a sense in which "Biblical preaching" may not be done by the "expository method." Nevertheless, *all truly expository preaching is indeed Biblical preaching*. Hence, in this volume, the reader should consider the two terms to be virtually *synonymous*.

Peter Lumpkins,
Managing Editor

A Collection of Essays on Biblical Preaching in Honor of Jerry Vines

Foreword

by David L. Allen

August 11, 1968 was a pivotal date in my life, though I did not know it at the time. On that day, my home church, West Rome Baptist Church in Rome, Georgia, called Jerry Vines to be her pastor. I was 11 years old. In his first year, there were 120 baptisms and 149 other additions to the church. For the next six years the church experienced phenomenal growth with Sunday School attendance exceeding 1000. Every service was like a revival service. From 1968 to 1974, under the superb, passionate expository preaching of the then unknown Jerry Vines, no less than three dozen men and women were called by God to full-time Christian service. One of them was a sixteen year old junior in high school. For a period of six months, I knew that God had been dealing with me about His call on my life. On November 18, 1973, I walked down the aisle at the conclusion of our Sunday night service and told my pastor God had called me to preach.

Later that night, after pizza and Coke at a local restaurant with several in our youth group, I returned home. I was too keyed up to sleep, so I went outside, lay down on the hood of dad's old Chevrolet Impala, and gazed up at the sky. The breeze played its haunting tune through the tops of the tall Georgia pines that studded our front yard. The words of a recent sermon from Dr. Vines ticker-taped across my mind. He was referencing 1 Corinthians 3:10-15 and 2 Corinthians 5:10 about how we all must stand at the Bema of Christ to give an account for our lives. Works of gold, silver and precious stones abide, but wood, hay and stubble is burned. Forever etched in my mind are these passionate words, "Some Christians will stand before the Lord in that day and press into the nail-scarred hands of Jesus the charred embers of a wasted life." I remember praying: "Oh God, don't let that be me." Jerry Vines' preaching marked me for life.

Jerry Vines entire 60 plus years preaching ministry is by his own admission John 3:16 in a nutshell. From small country churches in rural Georgia to the mega-church First Baptist in Jacksonville, Florida, and everywhere in between, Jerry Vines proclaimed the message of God's love for the world. When he began preaching at age sixteen, he had only one book in his library in addition to the Bible: George W. Truett's *A Quest for Souls*, an apt title and descriptive harbinger of one of the key motives which would drive a lifetime of preaching. However, like Truett, Vines was a topical preacher since that was the only kind of preaching he had ever heard.

But he soon discovered he was never satisfied with this approach. Through the influence of W. A. Criswell, Warren Wiersbe, and John Phillips, Vines learned there was a more excellent way: expository preaching. When he arrived at West Rome Baptist Church in the fall of 1968, his new found commitment to expositional preaching through books of the Bible would revolutionize a church over the next six years. From this launching pad, Jerry Vines' preaching would impact the Southern Baptist Convention and beyond.

When Vines left West Rome Baptist Church in the fall of 1974 to accept the pastorate at Dauphin Way Baptist in Mobile, Alabama, he wrote a letter to his new congregation in which he stated, "The preaching of the Word of God will be central in the ministry of the pastor ... The whole Word of God will be preached without fear or favor." It also stated, "Visitation to win the lost will be given top priority in all the activities of the church. The goal will be to evangelize the city of Mobile for Jesus Christ." These words express the marching orders which Jerry Vines lived by each day. Expository preaching and soul winning were his priorities.

In 1982, Vines became co-pastor with Homer Lindsey Jr. at the great First Baptist Church, Jacksonville, Florida. And the rest, as they say, is history. For the next quarter of a century, Dr. Vines preached expositionally through the entire Bible book by book.

Jerry Vines is known as a pastor, soul-winner, church builder, denominational leader, author, and many other things. But he is preeminently known for his preaching. Though one could focus on any one of these many areas of his kaleidoscopic ministry, this book first and foremost is an expression of appreciation to honor Dr. Vines for his preaching. In a culture where many preachers preach horizontally to felt needs — cotton candy, five ways to be happy sermons —Vines always preached vertically — extolling and exalting God before the people as the only One who could meet their needs through the Word of God. While some other preachers served up junk food, to dine at "Vines Place" every Sunday was to enjoy a full-course meal.

His preaching was intensely spiritual, but always perfectly Biblical and thoroughly practical. Like Ezra before him, "he blessed the Lord God" in his preaching and "all the people answered, Amen, Amen … and they worshiped" (Nehemiah 8:6). Unlike many modern preachers, Jerry Vines never endured the disgrace of having a sermon received with blank stares and feelings of boredom. Whereas some listeners wait for the end of the sermon as if it were bad weather to be endured until the sun shone once more, or relief after a root canal, people listen to a Jerry Vines sermon sitting on the edge of their seats and are disappointed when he decides to say no more.

Eloquent nonsense abounds in pulpits today. Sometimes it is not even eloquent. The eloquence of Vines' preaching lay not primarily in his wordsmithing abilities, but in his firm commitment to and exposition of the text when he preached. I admire him for the fact that he always looked at his Greek New Testament or the Hebrew Old Testament when studying a passage to preach. In a day when People's Magazine provides about as much sermon fodder for some preachers as the Bible, Vines' paramount commitment to expositional preaching is welcome tonic.

Audio and digital copies of Vines' sermons have traveled around the world providing encouragement to countless pastors and laymen. I smile when I think of how many Jerry Vines' points, illustrations, and other sermon material have been preached by preachers whose inspiration and information came from one of his sermons. His preaching has had a tremendous influence beyond the churches where he served as pastor. No one who has ever heard his famous sermon "Our Ascended Lord" first preached at the Alabama State Convention Pastor's Conference in 1976 will ever forget it. A week does not pass but that Dr. Vines receives some contact from someone around the world whose life has been touched by listening to that sermon. A turning point in the Southern Baptist Convention conservative resurgence came when Vines preached his famous sermon "A Baptist and His Bible" at the annual Southern Baptist Convention meeting in St. Louis in 1987. I was present and the hall was electric. No doubt the effect of that sermon contributed to Jerry Vines being elected president of the Southern Baptist Convention in San Antonio the next year.

At the encouragement of Paige Patterson, Jerry Vines wrote two books on the subject of preaching back in the 1980's which were widely read: *A*

Practical Guide to Sermon Preparation and *A Guide to Effective Sermon Delivery*, both published by Moody Press. Later these two books were revised and updated by Jim Shaddix and combined in one volume entitled *Power in the Pulpit*. This book has become a standard textbook and is used in many Bible colleges and seminaries. Vines has published numerous books of sermons and other studies throughout his illustrious career which continue to influence and impact not only the Southern Baptist world, but the broader evangelical world as well.

Preach the Word is not a biography or even a study of Vines' own preaching. This is a book about preaching. But more than that, this is a book about expository preaching. It contains a collection of essays by contemporary Southern Baptist preachers, pastors and scholars on Biblical preaching.

An introductory chapter by Emir and Ergun Caner provides a brief summary look into the life of Jerry Vines the preacher. Malcolm Yarnell explores the importance and priority of a simple Biblicism over against a theological model as a necessary premise for sound expository preaching. Johnny Hunt adds a testimonial chapter on the power of Biblical preaching.

O. S. Hawkins takes us into his study and provides practical advice on how to outline a text of scripture for preaching. Steven Smith's "Preach the Word: The Church's Necessity for 21st Century Survival" and Paige Patterson's "Preach the Word: God's Imperative for the 21st Century Preacher," combine to champion the cruciality of expository preaching today. Stephen Rummage reminds us that the true measure of success in Biblical preaching is not nickels and noses. Steve Lemke contributes a crucial chapter on a theology of Biblical Preaching, a topic in need of renewed reflection today. Adam Dooley and Mac Brunson provide important chapters discussing preaching from a pastoral perspective from their wealth of pastoral experience. Jeff Pennington keys in on Paul's admonition to Timothy that the preacher must also be about the business of winning souls for Christ. Finally, Steve Gaines addresses the subject of church growth and Biblical preaching.

Jerry Vine's life and ministry could be summed up in the words of the great reformer Martin Luther, "I simply taught, preached, wrote God's word … otherwise I did nothing … the Word did it all."

Part I:
The Preacher

A Brief Look into the Life of the Preacher: Jerry Vines

by Emir and Ergun Caner

*A*s Jerry Vines took his place to preach to the thousands assembled in St. Louis for the Southern Baptist Convention in 1987, little did he realize that his sermon, "A Baptist and His Bible," would literally shape the conversation among Southern Baptists for a generation. Baptists were enthralled in a debate over the veracity and authenticity of Holy Writ; indeed, Southern Baptists were warring over the very soul of their beloved convention and the spiritual path she would follow. The issue, the inerrancy of the Bible, had taken center stage in the Convention for decades and it now found its zenith during a 41-minute sermon by the Co-pastor of the First Baptist Church of Jacksonville, Florida. And the Lord had been preparing Dr. Vines for such a time as this.

Dr. Vines, whose rages-to-riches-in-Christ story in many ways personifies the quintessential Southern Baptist, did not waste a single moment of the limited time allotted, recognizing the significance of the hour. The future of the Southern Baptist Convention was at stake and its future would be decided forthwith. Preaching from the King James Version of 2 Timothy 3-4, the preacher, dressed in an unassuming grey suit, read his text and then stated, "Paul kinda sounds like a Baptist." Blending baptistic analogies like "little Billy Baptist" and "First Baptist Lystra" with Greek exposition, Vines, with his noticeable Georgian draw, walked the assembly through the text verse by verse. His message of simple Biblicism did not fall on deaf ears as applause and standing ovations rang out through the auditorium repeatedly during his message. In an instant he was the mouthpiece of thousands of Baptists who stood shoulder-to-shoulder with this self-acclaimed simple, country preacher.

During the message, Vines heralded a clarion call against what he termed "Destructive Criticism," a system of thought that placed doubts on the Bible and led to "faith-depleted schools, bankrupt denominations, and powerless churches."[1] Vines exclaimed, "For a man to touch the Word of God with irreverent hands and create doubt is like tampering with the medicine of a sick man."[2] Dr. Vines recognized that an undermining of Scripture would also chip away at a Christian's ability to evangelize a lost world. He stated, "Brethren, if you don't believe the book, you're out of business in the homes of lost people."[3] The message, it became obvious, was as much personal as it was prophetic. The life of this preacher was wrapped wholeheartedly in God's Word and the proclamation of its message of salvation. It was his life.

A Christian Foundation In Early Childhood

Charles Jerry Vines was born on September 22, 1937 in Carroll County, Georgia, a rural setting that his mother, Ruby, described as "way up on a hill in the country."[4] His grandfather, W. O. Johnson, was a country evangelist who spent hours teaching young Jerry about the premillennial return of Christ.[5] Vines himself manifested a strong desire for God's Word. He would regularly sit on the second pew in his church and copiously take notes on the preacher's sermons.[6] In 1946 Vines surrendered his life to Christ[7] and by 1953, at the age of sixteen, Vines accepted the call to preach.[8] The Vines family had a great reverence for pastors and when Jerry announced his call to his church, his father "came down and with tears said, 'You can count on me.'"[9] Vines' first sermon, "On to the Goal," was preached at the Shady Grove Baptist Church in Carrollton, Georgia, with less than a dozen people in attendance. The experience, although admittedly fearful, gave the young preacher confidence "of the power of preaching God's Word."[10]

The first two books in the young preacher's library were the Bible and George W. Truett's *A Quest for Souls*. These two books in many ways would hone the two key marks of Vines' ministry: a belief in the inerrancy of God's

Word and a dedication in sharing Christ with a lost world.[11] His passion for souls was confirmed when he won two brothers to Christ who were living in a housing project in his hometown. He reminisces, "When I led them to Christ, and then when I saw them baptized at the main church that Sunday night, it just absolutely put the fire in my bones. I mean, I found a joy there that I have never known and that I wanted to experience from now on, that I've never really gotten away from."[12]

College And Introduction To Liberalism

At the same time his love for the lost was growing, Vines matriculated at Mercer University, a school affiliated with the Georgia Baptist Convention. It was here on the Macon, Georgia campus that Vines gained a love for the Biblical languages as he majored in Christianity and double minored in Greek and Philosophy. His studies were of tremendous help to him as he was also a young pastor.[13] However, Mercer University also tested the young preacher as many of the faculty were adherents of higher criticism, a system that "demythologized" the Bible. Demythologization was a Biblical interpretation that removed the supernatural elements of Scripture —the "myth" according to German theologians such as Rudolph Bultmann (AD 1884-1976)[14] — for a more naturalistic, modern rendering of the text. Thus, learned professors who taught Vines were now questioning beliefs held by Vines since early childhood, including belief in creation, the Flood, miracles, and the very inspiration of the Bible.[15]

In a sermon nearly 50 years after his theological struggles at Mercer University, Vines shared with the congregation of First Baptist Church of Jacksonville about this crisis in his life:

> I had been brought up in a Bible-believing church. I had been taught that the Bible was the inspired Word of God. So, I went away to college to study to preach the Gospel. I remember my first classes. I went into classes where very intelligent, very highly educated men made statements like this: "Any man who says the Bible is without error is a fool." I heard statements like this: "You can't believe all the miracles really happened in the Bible."

And so, you see, this brought a crisis in my life. On the one hand, I had been taught by my pastor and my Sunday School teachers that the Bible was the inspired Word of God. Now, here were men with Ph.D. degrees saying, 'That's not true. What you have heard previously is not the case.'

And so, I came to a time of crisis in my life. I was going to a school in Macon, Georgia, and I remember as an 18-year-old freshman in college, I made my way one afternoon out to a park there in Macon, Georgia—Baconsfield Park. I went out there, and I remember kneeling out there in that wooded area, and I remember I had a copy of my Bible. I said to the Lord, I said, "Lord, I've been taught that this Bible is Your Word. I am now hearing that it is not Your Word, and, Lord, they are smarter than I will ever be, but, Lord, You have taught me. I have been taught by those I respect that the Bible is God's Word. I will take what they say by faith; I will believe that the Bible is inspired."[16]

Little did Vines know that the struggle he personally had with Holy Scripture would be a microcosm of an entire denomination's struggle about God's Word. His experience would prove invaluable when called upon years later to defend the Word against these Modernist voices.

Taking Major Steps In Short Time

With a firm conviction of faith and his call, Vines began serving churches in Georgia. As God blessed his first church, the Centralhatchee Baptist Church in Franklin, God led him to the Bethesda Baptist Church in Carrollton, Georgia, in 1957, at the tender age of twenty. In his third year at the church, the Lord decided to bless the young pastor in a way he did not expect. On Homecoming Sunday in May of 1960, Vines was preparing to preach on Jacob's Ladder. But as he has often said in the last 55 years, when Janet Denney attended the service that morning— it was Pastor Vines himself who fell off the ladder! He was immediately smitten by the sorority girl from the University of Georgia, and he ran to the back of the church after the service in hopes of shaking her hand. It would be another two months before they had their first date. The courtship was both difficult and immediate. The one hundred mile roundtrip between Carrollton and Atlanta was arduous, but happily short-lived. Their first date was on July 29, 1960. They were engaged less than a month later, on August 16, and married on December 17, 1960.[17]

Never one to let time waste, two weeks after their wedding, the Vines' moved to New Orleans, Louisiana, as Jerry began his graduate studies at the seminary. In Nancy Lee Smith's riveting "A Faithful Soldier," Janet spoke of her issues with adjusting to the life of seminary students who are young, newly married and impoverished: "A 32-foot trailer by eight feet wide. No air-conditioning in New Orleans. Then I became with child and deathly sick. I just about died. I really did. So, we had to leave and go to our first church."[18]

The couple left New Orleans to return to the pastorate in Georgia. Between 1961 and 1964, God grew the Vines' in both ministry and family. Jerry's first church upon their return was the Second Baptist Church in Cedartown, Georgia. While there, the Vines' celebrated the birth of their first child, Joy, in November of 1961. After moving to the Eureka Baptist Church in Carroll County, Georgia, the couple welcomed the birth of their twins, Jim and Jodi.[19]

Vines yearned to complete his seminary studies, but with family obligations and a growing preaching ministry in Georgia, he decided on an unusual solution. Each Monday, while leading Second Baptist in Cedartown, he would ride the train from their Georgia home to New Orleans, go to classes all week, and then ride the train again all night Friday. Arriving home early Saturday morning, Vines would spend all day Saturday on visitation, preach all services on Sunday, and then ride the train the following day west to Louisiana. During that year of solid, mind-numbing labor, God blessed the young preacher's commitment. In 1966 he received his Bachelor of Divinity, and saw the church baptize 110 people![20]

In 1967, God moved the Vines family to the First Baptist Church in Fort Oglethorpe, Georgia, and both the church and the family grew. Their fourth and final child, Jonathan, was born there. As noted by Jeffrey Pennington, this small chapter in Vines' ministry signified a major paradigm shift in his preaching. The topical sermon gave way to the expository method or as Vines himself describes the shift, the second period in his preaching ministry. Vines stated, "As I began to prepare expository sermons I made a marvelous discovery. My own ministry was completely changed and I become convinced of the value of expository preaching in the life of myself and in the life of the people to whom I preach."[21]

His continued popularity as a preacher and growing reputation as an innovative pastor led the West Rome Baptist Church to extend the call to Vines in 1969. The church leadership knew that their new pastor was going to spark a revival in their midst, but even they could not predict what the Lord would do. Over the next five years, they would see the church launch a radio program, a bus ministry, a deaf ministry, a flourishing children's church and a bookstore. Ironically, during one of the busiest periods of time in his ministry, Vines also earned his Doctor of Theology degree from Luther Rice Seminary. The growth of the church was so spectacular that it was noted that in just the first year of his ministry there, the church grew by almost three hundred additions.[22]

With Blessings Come Burdens

As many pastors can attest, sometimes the most prosperous ministries can also be the most troublesome. In 1974, Vines accepted the call to the Dauphin Way Baptist Church in Mobile, Alabama. It would mark a time of testing and blessing for the family. The explosion of growth at the church was almost immediate. In short order the church added services to meet the growing needs of the church. Virtually every week souls were being saved, and after just two years, the reputation of both the preacher and the church had grown to the point where Dr. Vines was elected president of the Alabama Pastor's Conference (1975) and President of the Southern Baptist Convention's annual Pastor's Conference (1976).[23]

Such blessings, however, often come at a heavy price. The time at Dauphin Way was not easy by any means. The growing church was a threat to the established power structure of the church and, through the years, Vines has often spoken of those days of testing. Between 1974 and 1979, the church averaged over 250 baptisms a year, yet some were troubled by their pastor's use of informal and revivalistic worship and even his "refusal to wear the traditional dark suits in the pulpit."[24]

Nonetheless God continued to bless Vines as the young man stood anchored to his conservative beliefs and expository preaching. In 1976 he preached a sermon at the Alabama Baptist Convention entitled "The Ascended Lord" that placed him in the pantheon of popular contemporary preachers. He was asked to preach that sermon all over the South, and, in 1977, before he was even forty years old, he was nominated for President of the Southern Baptist Convention. Though Vines lost since another candidate split the conservative vote and Jimmy Allen was elected, the firebrand from the Georgia countryside would become one of the most in-demand preachers of our time.[25]

A Ministry Of Healing And A Calling From A Friend

In 1980 Vines returned to the West Rome Baptist Church in an act of mercy. The church had fallen into a dispute that threatened to permanently divide the congregation. Many felt that their former pastor was the only man who could heal the schism. With patient preaching and a consistent emphasis on the main task of soul winning in a church, Vines was able to see the church return to health. By 1982, they had baptized 282 new converts into the fellowship.[26]

In early 1981, Vines received a phone call from one of his dearest friends with an unusual offer. Dr. Homer Lindsay Jr. had been the Senior Pastor of the First Baptist Church of Jacksonville, Florida since 1975. He was calling Vines to ask him to consider becoming his Co-Pastor. The Vines and Lindsay families were close friends, even taking vacations together, but Jerry felt the offer was just a good-natured jesture on Lindsay's part. A year later, Dr. Lindsay called again. This was not an unusual offer by Lindsay Jr. given the circumstances under which he became Senior Pastor at Jacksonville First. His father, Homer Lindsay Sr., had pastored First Baptist since 1940, and then in 1969, invited his son to join him as Co-Pastor. It was a ministry that suited all involved until Dr. Lindsay retired in 1975. Yet in the previous seven years, as Lindsay Jr. led as the sole pastor, the church had grown exponentially. Membership had gone from 4,500 to over 13,000. It was a ministry that demanded co-laborers in Lindsay's mind, and God was leading him to call his friend.[27]

Even Dr. Vines has admitted that such an arrangement was unique. Yet it would become a model of love and respect for almost twenty years. Both men possessed such complimentary characters and committed faith that they seemed to be completely in sync without even discussing matters. Until the death of Dr. Lindsay in early 2000, the two men preached and led side-by-side through one of the most prosperous periods in the history of the church. From 1982-1989, the First Baptist Church of Jacksonville, Florida became an epicenter of God's work. During that stretch they baptized an average of over 900 people a year, totaling 7,727. Sunday School attendance went from 4,747 in 1982 to over 6700 in 1989. The two men led by example. Both were directors in the age-graded Sunday School department. Both led weekly teams on visitation. By 1989, two thousand church members were trained to be leaders in Sunday School, and over one thousand people were regulars in church visitation. There was no secret to the growth. The commitment of the pastors and the church was simple and clear: evangelize through the Sunday School to reach every soul for Jesus Christ.[28]

A Ministry Of National Influence

As God continued to bless the church in Jacksonville, the pulpit ministry of Jerry Vines reached across the Southern Baptist Convention on a national scale. In 1984, Moody Press asked him to write a book chronicling his expository approach to preaching. The resulting book, *A Practical Guide to Sermon Preparation*, became such a popular work that Moody asked Dr Vines to write a follow up. In 1986, the subsequent book, *A Guide to Effective Sermon Delivery*, detailed the actual homiletical structure he employed in preaching. Over the course of the next twenty-five years, Dr. Vines has become a mentor in the fields of hermeneutics and homiletics to an entire generation of preachers through these books, which have been combined into one best-selling work and in use since the initial publication twenty-five years ago.[29]

With such a large influence on a national scale comes a larger responsibility. Since his initial foray into Southern Baptist denominational leadership, Dr. Vines had been working with Judge Paul Pressler, a Southern Baptist layman from Houston, Texas, and Dr. Paige Patterson, then President of The Criswell College in Dallas, Texas, to bring about the Conservative Resurgence.[30] From 1979, thousands of grassroots pastors united to bring Southern Baptists back to their conservative moorings. The inerrant and infallible nature of the Scriptures had been attacked over the course of decades following World War II, mostly among the academic world and denominational leadership. With the election of Dr. Adrian Rogers in 1979, this trend was slowed, and then reversed.[31]

At every juncture, Dr. Vines worked tirelessly and often at professional risk. The attacks by other Southern Baptists who did not share their conservative stance often surprised the leaders of the Resurgence, but it did not stop them. In 1984, Vines was asked to nominate Dr. Charles Stanley, Pastor of First Baptist Church Atlanta, Georgia, for president of the national body, which Stanley won on the first ballot. Vines served on the seminal SBC Peace Committee from 1985-1986. His 1987 sermon "A Baptist and His Bible" became the *Cri de Coeur* of the movement,[32] and in June 1988, he was elected to the first of two terms as president of the Southern Baptist Convention.[33]

The Final Pastoral Decades

The decade of the Nineties was distinguished by milestones in the life of Jerry Vines. The Jacksonville church baptized 8,902 people during the decade, and membership grew to over 26,000 by 1999, and their offerings totaled over $11 million. In 1999, the church was recognized for giving over one million dollars to missions.[34]

Drs. Lindsay and Vines led the church to build the present auditorium which seats nearly 10,000. During a time when countless churches are moving to the suburbs, the church decided to stay in the center of downtown, and built the entire facility debt-free. In 1999, Vines was appointed to the committee that would present the *Baptist Faith and Message* to the Southern Baptist Convention messengers. The Confession was affirmed and adopted at the annual meeting in Orlando in 2000, and represents the most cogent statements of Baptist doctrine and soteriology in America.[35]

The decade was not without struggle however. In 1994, Dr. Vines lost one of his mentors and heroes in the ministry when Jess Hendley died in February. As the decade came to a close, Vines and the church also struggled with the death of his beloved Co-Pastor, Homer Lindsay Jr. Almost exactly six years to the day from the loss of one of the greatest influences of his life, one of his dearest friends died on a Sunday night. The death of Dr. Lindsay placed the burden of leadership solely on Dr. Vines' shoulders. From 2000-2005, the church continued its evangelistic emphasis under his steady leadership. During those years the church baptized 3,449 souls and church membership swelled to over 28,000.[36]

As a new millennium dawned and a nation stood at the crossroads of political correctness and historical revision, Vines preached like the prophets of old. At the 2002 SBC Pastor's Conference meeting in St. Louis, Vines compared the life and ministry of Jesus Christ as the God-Man to Islam's prophet Muhammad. In the charged cultural atmosphere following the Muslim attacks on 9/11/01, Vines drew attention to Muhammad's marriage to Aisha when he was more than 50 years of age and she was only nine-years-old. The firestorm that followed would have caused other men to retract their statements quickly or go on an "apology tour." Though he had death threats after ABC Nightline aired the story, Vines never flinched. He stood his ground. Once again, the pulpit ministry of Dr. Jerry Vines was an example of unwavering commitment to the truth.[37]

On May 1, 2005, Dr. Jerry Vines announced his retirement during his morning sermon in his pulpit. Having been a pastor for over 45 years, Dr. Vines wanted to devote his life to writing and speaking around the world. Nine months later, he would answer the question so many pastors and preachers asked in the following months: how would Jerry Vines preach his final sermon? Fittingly, his last sermon as pastor was at the conclusion of the 20th Annual Pastor's Conference at First Baptist Jacksonville. On February 7, 2006, in a packed auditorium with over 10,000 people in the main room and thousands in overflow, Dr. Vines once again proved his reputation as an explosive expositor. Concluding his message on "Old Preachers Never Die," Vines broke out into song as he took the unprecedented step of slowly walking down out of the pulpit, down the center aisle. People began to stand, to see what was happening, but Dr. Vines' voice only grew stronger and clearer as he continued singing and walking, out the auditorium, through the foyer, out of the building and into an awaiting car.

If retirement means a slowed pace, then Jerry Vines is not retired. He and Janet moved back to Georgia, and he continues to preach. He is in such demand that churches will stay on a "waiting list," in case of the rare cancellation. His website is extremely popular, and his published Sunday School lessons, entitled "Vines by the Book," have become standard curriculum for many churches. He hosts national meetings that draw thousands, such as the John 3:16 Conference. While most men would sit back and enjoy the results of a fifty year pastoral ministry, Vines is only content looking forward. The churches he has served have baptized more than 23,000 people in his tenure, yet he continues with his burden to preach and train pastors to build evangelistic churches.

Through it all, Jerry Vines has quietly built a life of a consistent Godly influence. He has trained and been an example to young men across the globe, including these authors. One of his closest friends, Dr. Paige Patterson, perhaps said it best when Baptist Press asked him about Vines' impending retirement. Patterson said, "I wouldn't hesitate to say that Dr. Jerry Vines and Dr. Adrian Rogers were the two most important figures in the conservative movement."[38]

In the decade following his retirement into itinerate evangelism, Jerry Vines continues to study, prepare sermons and preach the Word of God innumerable times a year. Just to survive that life demands special precautions. But with Dr. Charles Jerry Vines, God also gave him a mental acuity to dissect the text and the gift of compassion, to speak into the lives of hurting pastors and broken churches. West Rome Baptist was not the only church to which he returned, and neither was it the only people Dr. Vines rescued from spiritual defeat and certain foreclosure. There are many of us— even those reading these very words— who have received a midnight phone call of encouragement, or an email of lift, or a hand written letter of love and kindness.

Long ago, his grandfather compared Charles Jerry Vines to the weeping prophet Jeremiah. In his grandson he saw those qualities of ironclad courage and gentle nurturing compassion. Half a century later, we are evidence of grandfather's discerning words. For us, and for our denomination, Dr. Jerry Vines has been our Jeremiah.

Preach the Word: A Personal Testimony to the Power of Biblical Preaching

by Johnny Hunt

*W*hat a great honor I have been afforded to be able to write a chapter in a book dedicated to and honoring Dr. Jerry Vines. Few men have had the influence on my life as this Gospel preacher. God has used him in my life as both friend and mentor. His preaching has not only motivated me, but I have found it to be extremely memorable. I can remember slipping into First Baptist Church Jacksonville when Dr. Vines was Pastor. He preached a message on the death of a conscience, about the life of King Herod. I am confident that I will never forget the power in which this message was delivered, as well as his use of incredible illustration. These show the Christ-honoring mind that God has placed in the person of Jerry Vines. The message impacted me in a way that continues to motivate me as a Gospel preacher. As far back as I can remember, Dr. Vines was always referred to as a country preacher with a big city church. This name stuck to him because of his commitment to care so deeply and passionately for the preachers of our Southern Baptist Convention. I am grateful that through the years of my ministry I fit within the ranks of those preachers who have been blessed and encouraged through Dr. Vines.

As we think about preaching the Word and consider a personal testimony to the power of Biblical preaching, I am grateful for the power and the authority of the Word of God. Early in my ministry, through the influence of men like Dr. Vines, I began to preach expositionally through books of the Bible. The book that Dr. Vines wrote on preaching happens to be one of the great motivators in my life. His book encouraged me not only to preach expositionally, but also to take a book at a time and teach our people. After 25 plus years of serving First Baptist Church Woodstock, I am confident that we can look into the lives of the people and see how God's Word has developed them. The proclamation of God's Word builds the people because of the marvelous truth of Hebrews 4:12, "For the word of God is living and powerful and sharper than any two-edged sword, piercing even to the division of soul and spirit, and of joints and marrow, and is a discerner of the thoughts and intents of the heart." In this passage, the writer of Hebrews reminds us that the Word of God is alive; I have found that it is so alive that it will get hold of the preacher. This text also speaks of the Word being powerful; it is not only the dynamite of God in written form, but it also has a particular dynamic that really moves the heart of both the sinner and the saint. The Word of God is sharper than a two-edged sword and, when proclaimed with the power of the Holy Spirit, cuts in a way that brings conviction and healing. The Word of God is piercing in that it does in the life of the hearer the same thing that the voice of Christ did in the life of the Apostle Paul when he was pricked by the Word. It is the discerner of thoughts and intents of the heart, dealing with both the mind and the motive of the hearer. This discerning work is encouraging when you realize that we can preach to the Christian family each week but yet know that the message pierces deep into the heart of the sinner to help him realize his need for God's Son. It is incredible that the preaching of God's Word can be comforting and nourishing, yet at the same time so convicting, piercing, and cutting. God's Word and the proclamation of it are the only way to build a Christ-honoring church.

When the Apostle Paul preached in the city of Thessalonica, the people heard the Gospel not only in word, but also in power and in the Holy Spirit and with much assurance. I am grateful that every time I have heard Dr. Vines preach he has preached not only with courage but also with confidence in the Gospel. There was a very clear assurance in the tone of his voice that he believed the proclamation that he was presenting. I will never forget a visitor coming through my Pastor's Reception after my 9:30 A.M. worship service a few weeks back. We introduced ourselves to each other, and I thanked him for being there that day. As we began to converse, he made me aware that he had been visiting for the last few months. His purpose for dropping by the Pastor's Reception was to inform me that he would not be returning. I felt that evidently someone had offended him, so I began to encourage him to let us help him with whatever was driving him away. It was then that the conversation became extremely enlightening. He shared with me that he did not believe the message of God's Word, but the attraction of our service was that he was confident that I believed the message. This served to remind me that it is not my job to convince the people that the message is God's message, but I must be convinced that it is God's message. I am grateful for the confidence with which Dr. Jerry Vines has preached the Gospel.

One of the great privileges that the Lord afforded to First Baptist Woodstock and myself was to have Dr. Jerry Vines for a teaching pastor at our fellowship for four years after his retirement from First Baptist Church Jacksonville. What an incredible blessing and privilege it was to have Jerry and Janet Vines with us during that time. Dr. Vines, on three or four occasions per year, would preach a three or four message sermon series to our congregation.

When I think of the power of the Word and Dr. Vines' ability to illustrate God's Word in such a memorable way, I will never forget his series on Heaven. In this series, he showed Biblically from so many different angles where we will spend eternity. In another series on John 3:16, Dr. Vines spoke in detail of the meaning of every word in the text and its authority. These are just a couple of examples and testimonies to the power of Biblical preaching. Any of you who ever had the opportunity of worshipping with the First Baptist Church Jacksonville family when Dr. Vines was pastor will quickly remember the power of the preaching from week to week in that pulpit. You will also remember, when the invitation was given, the many men and women and boys and girls, who came arm-in-arm with their friends as they brought them to Christ. They did this after being so convicted of their need to be evangelistic under the expositional and evangelistic preaching of Dr. Vines.

When it comes to Biblical preaching, a very challenging statement from God's Word is found in 1 Thessalonians 1:5. Paul says to the church at Thessalonica, "You know what kind of men we were among you for your sake." Paul's exemplary life served as a platform of integrity that all men could clearly see, establishing the creditability to have the right to be heard. I am grateful that when I think of a personal testimony to the power of Biblical preaching I can clearly see the life of Dr. Vines displaying integrity and creditability. These virtues seem to have added power to the platform that God has given him, whether in his preaching at home, in a Bible conference, or for our Southern Baptist Convention.

It is apparent that Dr. Vines spends much time in morning prayer, speaking to God before he takes the platform to speak to men. I have always appreciated and observed the life of personal holiness and commitment to Biblical discipline that is so evidenced in the life of this great preacher. It seems the more I consider God's touch on his life the more I see characteristics that any preacher would desire to be a reality in his own heart and life. Indeed, God has given this man of God the plan of God, as well as the hand of God, to proclaim boldly His Gospel so powerfully.

In one of our discussions with Dr. Vines, I remember him sharing with me that God had allowed him to preach through the entire Bible during his tenure at First Baptist Church Jacksonville. There is no doubt that he had seen Christ formed in the people. In Galatians 4:19, the Apostle Paul says, "My little children, for whom I labor in birth again until Christ is formed in you." This passage has always reminded me of a preacher in whom God has birthed a message in his heart. He literally labors over it, and as he approaches the Lord's Day, it is like a woman who has become pregnant and must give birth to her child. So many weeks God impregnated His Word, the Gospel, His Truth, in the heart of the preacher, and he could hardly wait to give birth to that message for the expressed purpose that Jesus Christ would be formed in the people. All of us who have observed the great First Baptist Church Jacksonville have seen men and women of great spiritual stature, which is a testament to the Word of God and the power in which it was proclaimed.

If there is one word that describes the powerful, Biblical preacher, it is the word "passion." This passion describes a certain zeal, a fire in the belly for the unquenchable desire to proclaim passionately God's Word. With this passion, we believe that as we admonish God's people with God's word, they will be radically changed by its message.

Following close behind the word "passion" is "compassion," which describes the preacher's love for the people he serves. This love is born first out of loving God with all one's heart, and second, out of a desire to see God's best in the lives of the people to whom you proclaim the truth. We do not proclaim a message because it is our duty, nor to just fill space in order to complete the time that has been allotted to us. This compassion comes from the conviction that we are indeed ambassadors sent from another place to represent the King of King and Lords of Lords. I have heard it said through the years that at the Judgment Seat of Christ the Lord would reward our service that was motivated by love, empowered by the Holy Spirit, and done for God's glory alone. Dr. Vines has modeled powerful preaching in a very personal way with these three themes at the heart of his messages.

When I reflect on memorable messages that were undoubtedly delivered in the power of God, I think of a message that Dr. Vines preached over 25 years ago at the Alabama Baptist State Convention entitled, *"From Glory to Glory."* Not only was I radically influenced, challenged, convicted, and encouraged by that message, but so were many others to whom I passed along copies of the message. The message became a testimony throughout our Southern Baptist Convention family of the power of God's Word by people hearing the message, both in person and by listening to the tape. Another message that all of us will remember was the one Dr. Vines preached at our Southern Baptist Convention when he was serving as the President entitled, *"Billy the Baptist."* I remember how Dr. Homer Lindsay sent a free copy of that sermon to all the Southern Baptist pastors throughout our Convention. The copies of the sermon were sent in such fashion because of the powerful way that Dr. Vines delivered that message.

I can still remember when I was a young pastor sitting on the front row at a Pastors' Conference of the Southern Baptist Convention when Dr. Vines preached a message entitled, *"Star-gazers."* I vividly remember to this day the heart of that message and how it so influenced and affected me to be a faithful witness for Christ. What a testament to the man of God and to the power of the Gospel. Paul exhorted Timothy to preach the Word, and if that message rang true in the first century, it is still true in the 20th and 21st centuries as Dr. Jerry Vines has boldly proclaimed the message of the cross without compromise.

I often consider what, in particular, so captivates me in powerful preaching, and what certainly comes to mind is the personality of the preacher who is delivering God's message and how personable he is. Dr. Vines has sought to be connected with all of his peers, regardless of the size of their church or educational background. You are always made to feel important in his presence which, once again, I believe magnifies that the Gospel that he preaches has not only been an agent of change in those who have heard it over the last fifty years; but, first and foremost, it also magnifies the radical, Christ-honoring change it has brought in his own life.

I have always been of the conviction that longevity is a key element in the development of powerful preaching and the building of a great work. Because of Dr. Vines' willingness to persevere and stay at First Baptist Church Jacksonville for so many years, which I believe he would acknowledge as being the best years of his life, God used him mightily through his consistent, biblical proclamation of God's Word to develop Christ-honoring followers. It has been said that if a man will stay in a church long enough, the personality of the church family will begin to resemble the personality of the pastor. First Baptist Church Jacksonville is known as a marvelous place to preach because the incredible receptivity and response you receive is an indication of the level of maturity that has been built into the people through the consistent, powerful proclamation of God's Word. We can all learn much by seeing and sensing what God has done in the life of the people as a direct result of powerful preaching, people heeding the Word of God, appropriating the resources of God's marvelous grace, and living out the Biblical mandate in their personal lives.

In seeking to wrap up my thoughts on a personal testimony to the power of Biblical preaching, I think of Dr. Jerry Vines and others who desire to really connect with those who are sitting under their ministry. A few descriptive words of their ministry that stand out most are: *passion, authenticity, content, careful exegesis, direction, and application.*

Passion, as I have mentioned, has been used to grip the listeners, and then it captures their attention when they know that you are so passionate about what you desire to share.

The second word is *authenticity.* The world doesn't need us to attempt to preach like someone else, but to be ourselves. Dr. Vines often taught me that I should *"milk all the cows that I can, but churn my own butter."* He helped me to realize the need to be authentic, genuine, and to be myself. It has been said that authenticity is one of the greatest traits that the younger generation in churches is looking for, and I believe that it spreads across every generation. The person who is speaking must be genuine and real.

The third word that comes to mind is the word *content;* not only to have studied the text in its context, but to have something to say — not just seeking to have cute stories, but to allow the Word of God and the text itself to drive the truth home to the heart of the listener. We must realize that the Word of God is living and active, and does a marvelous job of illustrating itself.

The next descriptive words are *careful exegesis*; to make sure that you say what the text says — letting the text speak for itself. God has chosen to honor His Word. The text becomes the truth that helps to explain itself as we continue to read and expound its truth.

Another word is *direction;* where you are taking us and how you would like for us to respond; what the point is of hearing the message. Dr. Vines is powerful in giving clear direction, and even the call for response.

Finally, *application* is a word that reminds us of the impact of the truth; and not only on our lives today, but on our lives, our family, our ministry, and all it pertains to for now and for all eternity.

I speak in personal testimony of how my own life has been influenced, encouraged, challenged, and convicted under the Biblical preaching of Dr. Jerry

Vines. Being so indebted to Dr. Vines, it is my prayer that I will never be the same in my preaching as a result of his influence. It is my prayer that I would continually be encouraged by him, seeing him as a model preacher and being motivated by his exemplary style of proclamation. Finally, it is my prayer that I will be challenged in my own heart to be a better preacher, as well as to pass on that which has been entrusted to me through this faithful servant.

"Simple Biblicism"
The Word of God in the Theology of Jerry Vines

by Malcolm B. Yarnell III

I will study [the Bible] on the basis of a 'simple Biblicism.'[1]" Thus proclaimed Jerry Vines in his most well known sermon. This was also the first sermon I ever heard preached by that humble master expositor of the Divine writ. While in the process of surrendering to a theological ministry, my beloved pastor, Wayne DuBose, now a Director of Missions in northwest Louisiana, encouraged me to be aware of the great intellectual warfare being waged among Southern Baptists. Brother Wayne understood that an appropriate resolution to the "battle for the Bible" was key, not only for the future of the Southern Baptist Convention, but also for the spiritual welfare and sound pedagogy of this aspiring theologian. Thus encouraged to investigate various sermons and writings and come to my own conclusions, I was profoundly and permanently shaped through Dr. Vines's convention sermon in Saint Louis, Missouri. As Adrian Rogers later noted, that June 1987 event generated "sympathetic vibrations in the hearts and lives of people to whom the Word of God is precious."[2] It certainly did with this young theologian.

In this essay I would like to tease out, from Vines's own writings, the outlines of the hermeneutical system he dubbed "simple Biblicism." It is a theological method, even a form of Christian piety, which helped shape my convictions regarding the formation of Christian doctrine.[3] First, a word about the term and its definition is required. "Biblicism" was first used in the English language with positive intent. In the early 19th century, evangelical authors spoke of Biblicism as a popular way to read Scripture. Biblicism was considered positively "vivacious" in its outworking even while it opposed overwrought theological speculation. Later, the Oxford Movement inspired by John Henry Newman led to a high-minded, negative evaluation of Biblicism. Many scholars and their students continue to treat Biblicism in a critical way, typically with a wrinkling of the nose, as if it were merely an expression of reductionist and legalist fundamentalism.[4]

As this essay will demonstrate, it is the prior, positive meaning that Vines has in mind, not the subsequent, obscurantist meaning. Biblicism, for Jerry Vines, is a way of reading Scripture that is open to and beneficial for all Christians but which demands the highest spiritual and intellectual commitment from the church's preachers and scholars. To arrive at a better understanding of Dr. Vines' simple Biblicism, we shall approach his theology of the Word of God through considering the Word of God in its integration, inspiration, interpretation, and indwelling.

I. *The Word of God Integrated*

The Word of God, according to Vines, is to be understood in a threefold way, in line with the Word's self-presentation. The Word of God is: living, written, and spoken. The "living Word" is the second Person of the Trinity, Jesus Christ, who is God come in the flesh to redeem humanity from sin on the cross. This living Word is the primary, though not exclusive, sense of the Word. The living Word may be and is both spoken and written, "I try to preach from the Word of God and I speak of the Word of God when I quote what the Bible has to say. But Jesus never had to quote from the Bible. Jesus Christ opened His mouth and it was the Bible. How do you like that? Every time He spoke it was not only the written Word[5], but it was the living Word speaking the written Word."

Vines is not saying that Jesus never quoted the Bible. He refuted those who would drive a wedge between the Divine Word and His written Word, as if Jesus did not respect the latter. Rather, Jesus Christ as the second person of the Trinity is the eternal *dabar* spoken and written by the Old Testament prophets and the eternal *logos* spoken and written by the New Testament apostles. The human Jesus was adept at utilizing the Old Testament and had the utmost respect for the Hebrew Bible. The human Jesus was the One to whom the Old Testament pointed and the One at the center of the New Testament. Vines' point is that Jesus as the living Word is eternally present in the spoken Word as it is recorded in the written Word. Phenomenologically, when the Christian preacher repeats the written Word, he is orally communicating the spoken Word, which itself is an instrument of the omnipresent but especially present living Word.

It is important here to note that the spoken Word is closely identified with the written Word and the living Word. Through this threefold integration of living Word, written Word, and spoken Word, Jerry Vines successfully holds off multiple errors simultaneously. First, *anti-Biblical liberalism* is corrected through keeping the written Word correlated with the living Word. Vines will not allow the thin end of the neo-orthodox wedge to be driven between the Word and Scripture, a wedge that may too easily transition into a full-blown critical and anti-supernatural liberalism.[6] Neo-orthodoxy was correct to see the living Word active in the written Word, but it erred in arguing that Scripture "became" the Word of God, for the Bible "is" the Word of God.

Second, *extra-Biblical enthusiasm* is corrected through keeping the spoken Word correlated with the written Word. Vines will not allow the preacher to assume that his own ideas and proclamations are necessarily to be identified as the Word of God simply because he has quoted the Word of God at some point in his sermon. The issue of revelation is too important to leave for men to surreptitiously identify their own innovative ideas as God's revealed will. The spoken Word must be based in and remain tethered to the written Word in order to be identified with the Word of God. Indeed, Dr. Vines more often relied upon a twofold definition of the Word of God, as "living" and "written."[7] His typical dual affirmation, as opposed to the more rare trifold meaning, occurred most likely because he understood the preacher's "speaking" of the Word to be entirely dependent upon the written Word, itself the expression of the living Word.

Third, *sub-Biblical fundamentalism* is corrected through keeping the living Word and the spoken Word correlated with the written Word. Vines often echoes the high regard that fundamentalist and Reformed theologians share with conservative Baptists for the written Word. He is, however, careful not to allow the written Word to become a cipher for a legalism that reduces the Word of God to mere commands. A fundamentalist treatment of the Divine commands may accidentally substitute human innovation for Divine intent. For similar reasons, Vines is careful not to allow the Bible to be used doctrinally in such a way that it minimizes the meaning of the text and the central importance of God as love and Jesus Christ as Lord.[8] He opposes the Reformed systematization of Scripture, because he sees it undermining the message of Scripture. As he wrote glowingly of the heart-warming message of Scripture in opposition to Calvinist speculation, "John 3:16 is a simple Biblicism which reveals the mind, the heart, and the will of God."[9] Contrary to some fundamentalist and Reformed treatments of the Bible, Scripture is living and active, highly personal and intimately relational, even as it also relays the authoritative commands and doctrines of the Lord for His disciples.

A moving portrait of this dynamic yet structured threefold relationship—the living Word and the written Word along with the faithful speaking of that Word—may be gained through hearing Vines wax eloquent on the unique relationship between the living Word and His written Word, the Savior and His Scripture:

> Of course [the Bible's] central personality is alive. When you read the personalities of other books they lie dormant upon the pages of that book. They are lifeless characters. They are fictitious. They never exist. They have no life-giving power in them. Yet, dear friends, when you and I open this Bible, this special book, the Bible, we are brought face to face with its central personality, the Lord Jesus Christ. And this living Lord Jesus, when we open the pages of the Bible and read about Him, literally steps off the pages of the Bible into this world, and steps off the pages of the Bible into a church, and off of its pages into a heart and into a life. Because you see, friends, this Bible, the written Word of God, introduces us to Jesus, the Living Word of God, and you come face to face with the living Lord Jesus Christ. No other book in all the world can do what this living book, the Bible, is able to do.[10]

Jesus Christ is not tangentially related to Scripture, either closely, as in neo-orthodoxy, or distantly, as in its acidic neighbor, liberalism. Jesus

Christ is not reduced to a mere figure, even if an instrumental one, as in fundamentalist and scholastic Reformed readings of Scripture. Jesus Christ is not supplemented by extra-Biblical revelations, as in enthusiastic abuses of Scripture. Jesus Christ, the Lord of creation, is active within and through Scripture, encountering the human being personally, who hears Him speak through the writings as the preacher proclaims the Word, encouraging the sinner to repent and believe in Him. The Word of God is integrated, beginning with the living Word, settled in the written Word, active through the speaking of the Word.

II. The Word of God Inspired

In the preaching of Dr. Vines, the Word of God is closely identified with Scripture, because God breathes the Bible. The primary purpose behind his famous sermon, "A Baptist and His Bible," was that it "be used of the Lord to create confidence in God's supernaturally, verbally, totally inspired Word."[11] That sermon was based upon II Timothy 3:14-4:13, particularly 3:16a, and was divided into three points: the intention of the Bible, the inspiration of the Bible, and the implications of the Bible. The intention of the "sacred Scriptures" was to bring about the conversion of sinners: "to make wise unto salvation."[12]

Vines' discussion of the inspiration of Scripture first prompted him to express publicly his appreciation for the teaching of his seminary professors. Their lectures dismantled the higher critical method and exalted "simple Biblicism." The reason for this move away from a hyper-scholarly criticism and toward an intentional humility before the words of the Biblical text was that Scripture described itself as *theopneustos*. This Greek word is "a verbal adjective used in a passive sense. The emphasis is that God alone is the agent in the Bible's inspiration. The Bible is the product of the creative breath of God. "God-breathed." That's the best way to translate it. Not man-breathed; "God-breathed." Thus, in the dynamic act of breathing, God creates that which we call "the Bible."

This Divine activity of inspiration carries with it a threefold implication. First, that Scripture is "God-breathed" indicates that inspiration is supernatural. As God breathed life into humanity, so He breathes life into the Bible, making it a living book. "The book pulsates with life." This Divine giving of life to a human book does not mean that the human element is removed from Scripture. Rather, Scripture has a "dual authorship." The personalities of the human writers are not lost. The Bible's composition by men inspired by the Holy Spirit is compared to "a vessel gently carried along by the wind." The Holy Spirit speaks by the mouth of these human writers. This dual authorship is analogous to the simultaneously Divine and human natures of the one person of Jesus Christ.

Like Christ, who was "touched by our humanity, but not tainted by our depravity," so the Holy Spirit "superintended" the human writers, "so that what they wrote was without error." The fundamental doctrine of inspiration by the Holy Spirit of God, therefore, necessarily entails the inerrancy of Scripture. The Spirit of God in His perfection maintains the perfection of the text that He inspired the authors to write. This perfection extends to matters of salvation, of science, and of history. While the Bible is not primarily intended to be a book of science or a book of history, but a book of salvation, it speaks truly when it touches upon science and history. For instance, while the virgin birth and the resurrection are primarily theological claims, they indicate historical and scientific factuality are coordinate to theological truth.

The second implication of Divine inspiration is that it is verbal. It is the written word, the *graphe*, which is God-breathed. Vines discounts the claim by some that it is the thoughts of Scripture, rather than its words, which are inspired. Such a claim is ludicrous, for "Words are the vehicles of thought." There are no thoughts that come apart from their expression in words. Words are, therefore, necessary, but words are not to be understood merely as coldly logical statements. The words of Scripture—from "justification" and "sanctification" to "faith," "love," and "hope"—are soothingly beautiful. There are explicit affirmations in Vines's preaching that aesthetics remain an important aspect of truth. "Sing them over again to me, wonderful words of life. Let me more of their beauty see, wonderful words of life." [13]

At this point, Vines makes one of his most powerful arguments by appealing to the teaching of the Lord Jesus Christ Himself. Before and during the inerrancy controversy, some theologians pitted Christ against Scripture, thereby undermining the latter's truthfulness,[14] but Vines showed that Christ Himself was meticulous regarding the truthfulness of His words, of

Scripture's words. "Did Jesus teach verbal inspiration?" In Matthew 4:4, the Lord said we live "by every word that proceeds out of the mouth of God." In Matthew 24:35, the Lord asserted, "My words shall not pass away." In Matthew 5:18, neither the smallest Hebrew letter nor the smallest part of a letter "shall under no circumstance ever pass from the law till all be fulfilled."

The third implication of the Pauline doctrine that "All Scripture is God-breathed" is that inspiration is total. Citing the universally revered Herschel Hobbs, Vines agrees that *pasa* means "all." Hobbs said, "It means that every single part of the whole is God-breathed." Vines agreed, "That's where I stand. That's where Southern Baptists have always stood." The problem that Southern Baptists now face originated with destructive criticism in Enlightenment Germany, then made its way to America through Northern evangelicalism, "leaving a trail of stripped denominations, faith-depleted schools, and powerless churches." The "old thief" of doubt about God's Word had its primary appeal among those who desired intellectual respectability.

Against such scholarly hubris, which draws upon criticism, feeds upon cynicism, and issues forth in heresy, Vines placed the Bible in "the hands and hearts of simple believers." The priesthood of believers is opposed to the elitist priesthood of the scholar. Taking Clark Pinnock directly to task for his statement that "Adrian Rogers does not really know the Bible and Roy Honeycutt does," Vines claimed that the preacher (Rogers) and the professor (Honeycutt) should not be pitted against one another; they should "be in partnership with one another." The Bible is a book "for common men" as well as scholars.

Dr. Vines was not arguing that scholarship is unnecessary for the study of Scripture. As we shall see, his claims and his practices were quite the opposite! His sermons demand the deepest attention from the discriminating intellect. What he was arguing is that the study of Scripture must begin with "a decision of the heart, not of the head." Only after the matter of Lordship is settled is the scholar ready to approach the Bible for detailed study. "The matter of the total inspiration of the Bible must be decided on the basis of lordship, not scholarship." But once the inspiration of Scripture is affirmed, then all the tools of scholarship come into play in "simple Biblicism":

I will study my Bible with more reverent, faith-building methods. I will study it textually, historically, grammatically, contextually, theologically, and practically. I will study it on the basis of a "simple Biblicism" which never calls into question the supernatural, verbal, or total inspiration of the Bible. Let the critics pick over the bones of the Bible. Bible-believing Baptists will continue to feast on the meat of the Word.[15]

III. The Word of God Interpreted

Once the inspiration of Scripture, and its resulting inerrancy, were established, Vines could turn to applying the Bible. However, before arriving at the application of Scripture, we should take a moment to examine in more detail his method of interpretation. As noted above, Vines correlated his method with "simple Biblicism," which is studying Scripture, through the eyes of faith, "textually, historically, grammatically, contextually, theologically, and practically." These six aspects of "simple Biblicism" are the human means for proper interpretation. The theological means for interpretation are assumed by Vines to be the Word of God and the Spirit of God appropriated by faith.

Textually: The method pursued in the sermons of Dr. Vines indicates that the scriptural text is the key to its own interpretation. The Word is composed of words, so words must be taken with utmost seriousness. "Words are vehicles of thought which reveal my mind and heart to you." As such, these vehicles are necessary for the conveyance of meaning. This is true among human beings, as well as for God in His communication with human beings. The living word, Jesus Christ, is significantly God's "Word of explanation"[16] to men. "God wanted us to know what He felt in His heart toward us." Thus, "He sent His Son to be the Word of explanation."

This theological commitment to the Biblical text as the Word of God is the reason behind Vines' consistent referral in his sermons to the Biblical text. Although Vines will use history, theology, and experience to explain and illustrate, his sermons are tethered to the words of the text, allowing the text's own organization and own definitions to shape, to drive, and to provide the primary content for the sermon. Jerry Vines is the expository preacher extraordinaire, because he believes the Bible is the inspired, inerrant, authoritative, written Word of God.

Historically: Dr. Vines is committed to a proper understanding of the Scripture-related events as historical in nature. The "living Word" is both eternal and historical. "This One who commenced history is the same One who controls history. And He is the same One who will return and will consummate history. So we are looking at the Jesus of yesterday." Jesus Christ, as the Lord of all time, is "the past Jesus, the Jesus of history," "the present Jesus, the Jesus of reality," and "the perennial Jesus. He is the Jesus of eternity."[17] Because the living Word is so tightly integrated with the written Word, then the Bible's history, too, is important.

Moreover, if the events of Scripture are not true historically, or "literally," then the faith itself is in vain. "If His return is not literal, then the ascension was not literal. If the ascension was not literal, then the resurrection was not literal. If the resurrection was not literal, then it is all over and Christians may as well just close their Bibles and go home."[18] Therefore, for the sake of the integrity of the Christian faith, the history of the contents of Scripture must be taken literally. This works itself out in a number of ways, including the deep knowledge that Dr. Vines displays, for instance, about the geographical, historical, and theological significance of the various mountains of Israel.[19]

Another instance of the importance of history is that the historical purposes within Scripture must be taken seriously. For instance, Romans 10 is interpreted not as a philosophical treatise on salvation, though it is theological, but as Paul's discussion of the historical importance of Israel and of the salvation available to the Jews. Salvation for the Jew is "exceptionally desirable," "entirely possible," and "especially available." Only while taking such Biblical history seriously should one then move to the text's theological treatment. Salvation for the Jew is the literal purpose of the text; while it reflects upon salvation for the Gentiles, it does so derivatively.[20]

Grammatically: Referral to the grammar of the original languages is amply evident within the sermons of Dr. Vines. Indeed, it could be claimed that his exegetical perception of especially the Greek New Testament is unparalleled among modern preachers. This focus on the grammatical details of the text extends to every word of a passage. It also informs his every theological interpretation of a passage. The grammatical construction of a passage, in turn, provides the structure and flow for the sermon. While the priority of expositional structure will be treated elsewhere in this volume, it is worth reviewing another example of how the original languages of Scripture shape Dr. Vines's preaching.

In his sermon on John 3:16, Vines appeals to three linguistic referees for the meaning of *houtos*, "so." Bauer, Arndt, Gingrich, and Danker's Greek lexicon translates it as a "demonstrative adverb." Thayer's lexicon translates it as "an adverb of degree." In agreement with the MacArthur Study Bible, Vines then proclaims, "There are volumes in that little word. God's love is not like a trickling stream; instead it is like a flooding river. It is not like a leaky faucet; instead it is like a bottomless ocean. … God's love is a reservoir that never runs dry!" He then proceeds to discuss the object of the verb, as well as every word in the subject passage, in just as much clarity and detail. A single word is filled with import when taken seriously in its Biblical and historical context.[21]

Contextually: The idea of context for Vines primarily concerns the canonical context and the canon's historical use of Biblical words. Extrabiblical context and grammatical use may be helpful, but they are secondary in importance to Scripture's own context and use. This requires an awareness of the place and role of a word in its sentence, paragraph, and particular book, as well as in the entire canon. He commonly refers to the various places and uses of words within the Bible.

For instance, with regard to the relation of the believer and the world, Vines demonstrates that in John 17, the relationship is complex and nuance must be retained. The series of phrases that Jesus uses must be set alongside one another. Christians are called "out of the world" spiritually, even while they remain "in the world" physically. Christians are, moreover, reminded that they are "not of the world," even while they are "sent into the world." The word "world" is used in several different ways in Scripture, and such diversity must be kept in mind while interpreting Scripture.

Theologically: The theological importance of Scripture for Dr. Vines should already be evident. Dr. Vines allows Scripture to shape all of his theological teachings. This is true with regard to revelation, salvation, and eschatology, among other doctrines, as a cursory reading of this chapter demonstrates. It is informative for today's discussions over such theological systems as Calvinism how the text's grammar and context shapes theology for Vines, in spite of the popular systems. Scripture must shape systematic theology; systematic theology must never mold Scripture to its preferences.

For instance, in what is perhaps his second-most important sermon, from a contemporary perspective, Vines touches upon theology proper through his treatment of John 3:16. Vines cites 1 John 4:8 for his bold claim that, "The fundamental assertion about God in the Bible is 'God is love.'"[22] He then moves to a consideration of how God "so loved" the world. "The verb is a first aorist, active, indicative verb. More specifically, the verb is not an ingressive aorist, which would suggest a time when God began to love. The verb is also not a cumulative aorist, which would indicate a time when God will decide to love. The verb is, however, a constantive aorist, which emphasizes God's eternal, constant, total love." Dr. Vines permits the scriptural context and grammar to drive his theology, rather than vice versa. With such a grammatical emphasis on love as Divine and eternal in the text, as interpreted by Dr. Vines, it is easy to discern how rejection of the New Calvinism, especially in light of John Piper's presentation of a self-centered God, could arise.

Practically: Dr. Vines often draws on personal experience to understand how the Word relates to human beings in practice. However, his reflective method of simple Biblicism entails allowing the Word to shape the interpretation of experience. The experience is not the instrument for shaping the interpretation of the Word. For instance, frustration with putting together complex models is a practical matter that is used by Vines to call Christians back to reading the Bible. "When all else fails, read the instructions."[23] Therefore, even his practical illustrations refer the listener back to the priority and sufficiency of the Biblical text for the beginning and continuance of the Christian life. The Word's interpretation is a function of the Word itself.

IV. *The Word of God Indwelling*

Dr. Vines believes that the entire Trinity is involved in the salvation of souls through the indwelling of God. With reference to his favorite character, "Billy Baptist," he asks, "How was Billy saved?" "He came to the church, heard the Word preached, was convicted by the Holy Spirit, and believed the truth. And he was saved!"[24] The Father is the beginning of salvation to eternal life. He is fundamentally love and demonstrates this love in history to humanity through the cross and resurrection of His Son. "It begins with a God who has no beginning and ends with a life that has no ending."[25] Complex speculation regarding Divine sovereignty and its relation to human responsibility does not hold a fascination for him. "A sovereign God has given every person the faculty of faith and a will to exercise it. This does not rob God of His sovereignty."[26]

As with the Father and the Spirit, the Word is active in the salvation of souls. The Word of God as living as Jesus Christ. Echoing Chalcedonian Christology, Vines says that He is pre-existent, co-eternal with God, co-existent with God, and co-equal with God. He is the "life" available for all men and the "light" in every man. Every man needs, in addition, the "light of Conversion," which is available only in Jesus Christ, although "light" is also used in reference to the Scriptures and the Spirit.[27] The integration of the written Word with the living Word extends thereby into integration with the Trinity through the Holy Spirit.

While the Word is living in the person of Jesus Christ, the written Word is also "living." The Bible is alive in the conversion of people, who—like Augustine of Hippo, Martin Luther, and Charles Haddon Spurgeon—come to the truth through the reading of the Bible. The Word is alive and leaps from the Bible to indwell the human heart. "That one word taken into your heart today can transform your life and you can walk out of here never again the same individual. The Bible is a special book because it is a living book." The written Word is, moreover, "energizing." The author of Hebrews "is saying there is inherent power in the Bible. There is energizing power in the Bible. The Bible does something on the inside of an individual. There is power in the word of God to work in a human heart." The Bible's indwelling work is to convert, to comfort, and to cleanse. Perhaps one reason that Vines is so adamant about the Word's power to convert is that his own conversion came through reading the Bible, too.[28]

With his doctrine of the indwelling Word of God, Vines brings together the intellectual and moral aspects of faith. Yes, Christ transforms human lives through words, but while some have the "facts," they also need the "fire." What the two disciples on the road to Emmaus needed "was a good, old-fashioned heart-warming experience with the living Lord." They had the facts, but not the fire. The Gospel facts of Christ's death and resurrection had not as yet "gripped them." Such integration of the "heart" with the "head" requires the Holy Spirit. This leads him to consider the problem of higher criticism. "The critic of the Bible can accumulate a lot of facts about the Bible but he will never really understand the message of the Bible. It has to be spiritually discerned."[29] Over against such liberal criticism (and later, Calvinist speculation), with its focus upon the head, Vines emphasizes the eternal need of the human heart to invite Jesus in to be Lord.

The Word of God is not only instrumental for the beginning of salvation in conversion; it is also instrumental in sanctification and glorification. The history of Christianity also demonstrates the priority of Scripture for the Christian life. Christians struggled to believe and live properly until they had the Word of God in their own tongue. However, the availability of the Word must be matched by its reading. The Word is to be read in a person's "quiet time" and in public worship. The Word is the "absolute" standard for what is true and false. "God works on our lives by truth," and the Word is His instrument. Not only must the Word be available and read, it must be assimilated and become the instrument God uses for our sanctification.[30] The Word of God is ultimately the "word of salvation." As such, "He calls His church to global missions," so that the Word will go forth and offer salvation to any who believe.[31] From personal conversion to the mission of the church, the indwelling Word of God permeates and empowers the Christian life.

The doctrine of "simple Biblicism" in the hands of Jerry Vines is simultaneously simple in its reverence for the Word of God and beautifully complex in its passion for the details of the Divine writ. According to Vines, the Word of God must be doctrinally integrated, recognized as fully inspired, and properly interpreted, and the Word of God will personally indwell believers. This is the legacy of Jerry Vines for the doctrine of the Word of God among Southern Baptists and contemporary evangelicals. His doctrine is fully my own as well. Thank you, Dr. Vines, for preaching to us theologians with your heart as well as your head.

Part II:
The Preached Word

The Preaching Event: A True Baptist Distinctive

by O. S. Hawkins

It has been my privilege to preach for decades behind Baptist pulpits across the world. My years in the pastorate took me from the plains of Southwestern Oklahoma, to the cosmopolitan resort of Fort Lauderdale to the concrete canyons of downtown Dallas. There for 100 years Dr. George W. Truett and Dr. W. A. Criswell expounded the "unsearchable riches" from, arguably, the most famous pulpit of the 20th century.

Our Baptist pulpits are rich in history and heritage. When I was a boy, my mother cooked every meal in our home in the same old cast iron skillet. Someone once gave her a new Teflon skillet but she never used it. She continued to cook breakfast, lunch and dinner in the same old skillet. And, things seemed to taste better when they were cooked in it. I am convinced it was because that old skillet had years of "build up" in it. There is a sense in which most every Baptist pulpit is like that old skillet; it has years of "build up."

The pulpit in a Baptist church is almost always on center stage. It is there to make the statement that central to Baptist worship is the preaching of the Book of God to the people of God. One can walk into the auditorium of a Baptist church anywhere in the world and the pulpit is there to signify the centrality of Gospel preaching in the Baptist tradition.

Living in this new millennium, preaching is facing its greatest challenge. We are the "prefix generation." We describe many things in our contemporary culture with the use of the prefix. For example, we use the prefix "mega" repeatedly. We have megabytes, megabucks, megachurches, and even mega-dittos. One of the prominent and popular prefixes of today is "eco," as in ecotone or ecosystem. An econtone is a technological word from the field of biology which describes a particular place where two ecosystems merge and blend together. I first heard of the word while living in Fort Lauderdale, Florida. There is a particular place there where the intercostal waterway and the New River come together and form an ecotone. The salt water from the Atlantic Ocean flows into Port Everglades and into the intercostal waterway. From the Everglades just west of the city the fresh water flows through the river making its way toward the ocean. At the particular place where the salt water and fresh water merge together an ecotone develops. Ecotones are places of tremendous possibilities. Often fish nestle there to lay their eggs. However, ecotones can also be very problematic to those who engage themselves in the battles of ecology.

In this new millennium our culture is in the midst of its own ecotonic stage. Two worlds are merging and blending together at the same time. One is a modern world and the other is a post modern world. The world in which most of us have been educated is history. All the cumulative knowledge of world history will double in the next five years. We are in a post-modern era which in itself can be a time of tremendous possibility for the church of the Lord Jesus Christ or a time of tremendous problems for those who allow the contemporary culture to dictate their approach to the truths of the Gospel message.

The preaching experience is in the midst of its own ecotonic period. It remains to be seen whether it will prove to be helpful or hurtful to the proclamation of the Gospel message. In the midst of this particular period of time there has arisen a new wave of preaching enthusiasts who are advocating an approach to proclamation that is foreign to the apostolic model. They have done their research, written their books, advanced their newsletters, promoted their tapes and seminars, and a new generation of young preachers seems to be influenced by their "findings" and persuasions. These modern church growth gurus have done their "marketing" and have returned to tell us that if we have any hope of penetrating the minds and hearts of our contemporary culture we must give them what they "want" to hear. Therefore, the modern approach to preaching is one of accommodation with a subtle, yet strong, emphasis on avoiding four specific distinctives that have been historically central to the Baptist preaching event.

There is a blatant emphasis today to *avoid context*. Many young preachers are being instructed to preach "topical" sermons on felt needs or wants and to avoid paragraph-by-paragraph, verse-by-verse, exposition. That is, one should select a topic related to a felt need and, if possible, find a Scripture to support it. This approach encourages the implementation of not only the latest secular communication principles but also success motivational techniques as well.

Secondly, a new generation of preachers is subtly being influenced to *avoid confessions*, that is, doctrinal truth. We are being told that the men and women we are trying to reach do not want to hear of Bible doctrines and making much of them will stunt church growth. Being dogmatic on matters of doctrine is "out" in contemporary preaching technique.

Not only is there a subtle emphasis in our day to avoid context and to avoid confessions but we are also being encouraged to *avoid controversy* from our pulpits. This accompanies a kinder, gentler approach to preaching that is tolerant of other people's views so as not to be offensive to them. Thus we find fewer and fewer pulpits taking clear Biblical stands on the social and moral issues such as abortion and homosexuality which plague our contemporary culture. The salt seems to be losing its savor and tragically it is emanating from the pulpit.

Finally, a generation of young preachers is being encouraged to *avoid confrontation*. Fewer and fewer pulpits in the western world are calling for men and women to take personal responsibility for their sin and make a public pledge of their faith to the one who said, "Confess me before men …" (Matthew 10:32). There is little emphasis upon confrontational evangelism today whether it is personal in the parlor or public from the pulpit. This particular and, unfortunately, popular approach to non-confrontational proclamation of the Gospel is what has led many churches to cease the public invitation and has led to only superficial mission involvement around the world.

One young Baptist pastor is quoted in a Baptist Press news release saying, "We have done one walk-the-aisle public invitation, and some of our folks were very uncomfortable with it because we promoted ourselves as being a church that is non-threatening. I don't think we will ever do it again."[1] Can anyone imagine Peter, James, Paul, or any of the apostolic pastors advertising their church as being "non-threatening?" Simon Peter preached the church's inaugural sermon and in the body of his message he cried out, "You with the help of wicked men have nailed Him to a cross" (Acts 2:23). Then at the end of the message he pleaded "with many other words" (Acts 2:40) for them to come openly and unashamedly to identify with the Lord Jesus Christ. The same Baptist Press release carried the words of a young North Carolinian pastor who also boasted about his non-confrontational approach saying, "We don't violate their emotions by singing four verses of "Just as I Am" and trying to manipulate them." The multiplied hundreds of thousands of men and women who will be in heaven because of the preaching and confrontational ministry of Billy Graham are certainly thankful he concluded his messages with an appeal to come to Christ as the choir sang, "Just As I Am."

The Biblical pattern of proclamation and church growth is in diametric opposition to these modern philosophies. One says we are to "market the church" by finding out the "wants" of the people and then tailoring our church programs to meet these "wants" and to avoid context, confessions, controversies, and confrontation in our preaching so as not to appear offensive to our hearers. The Biblical pattern is plain. We are to "church the market," that is, to take the gospel into the marketplace itself with an apostolic pattern of confrontational, confessional contextual, and sometimes controversial way which seeks to meet the "needs" of the human heart and not its "wants." In the Book of Acts we find that Bible preaching was central to the task of evangelizing and congregationalizing through the local church. When the church's emphasis centers upon the "wants" of the human heart, it turns inward. However, when it follows a New Testament pattern and centers on the "needs" of the human heart, it turns outward and the preaching event takes its proper place of priority.

One of the primary reasons the blessing of God has rested upon the Baptist church in the past century is the priority placed upon the preaching experience. Baptist churches and Bible preaching have, in the past, been synonymous. We have given emphasis to the apostolic pattern found in Peter's first recorded sermon on the temple mount on the day of Pentecost recorded in Acts 2 and in Paul's first recorded sermon at Pisidian Antioch recorded for all posterity in Acts 13. A careful analysis of each of these Bible messages reveals a balance in their preaching. They both follow a pattern which Paul later outlined to his young preacher understudy, Timothy. Paul instructed Timothy, and us, saying, "All Scripture is given by inspiration of God, and is profitable for doctrine, for reproof, for correction, for instruction in righteousness, that the man of God may be complete, thoroughly equipped for every good work" (2 Timothy 3:16-17). There are four characteristics that should be applied to every Gospel message in a balanced way. A Bible sermon should have in it an element of doctrine, that is, it should not shy away from the great truths of the Bible. It should reprove sin. It should correct false paths. And, it should have an element of instruction in righteousness which helps the hearer to apply to his or her life the Bible truths they have absorbed. Balanced preaching of God's word provides a road map for men and women journeying through life. The "doctrine" of salvation found in the Lord Jesus Christ enables one to get started on the right road. Along the way we may get off the path by rebellious acts of our own will. It is then that the Bible serves to "reprove" us in our sin. However, it does not leave us in reproof. It is also profitable for "correction." It serves to correct our way so that we will not get off on the same side street again. Finally, it is profitable to "instruct in righteousness" so that once on the right road and headed toward our final destination we may be being conformed to the image of Christ along the way. An effective and balanced ministry of the Word of God does all four of these things Paul mentions to his young understudy, Timothy.

The appeal is for a balanced ministry of God's word. Some pulpit ministries go to seed on "doctrine." Even though they are orthodox in their beliefs and doctrinally sound they seldom reprove sin, correct false paths, or instruct in righteous Spirit-filled living. Consequently, such churches are dead and dying. Others tend to go to seed on "reproof." They think their primary God-given call is to reprove everyone in their sin with a self-righteous pointed finger of accusation. They never teach Bible doctrine or instruct in righteousness and are puzzled as to why their churches continue to dwindle in number. Still, others go to seed on "correction" to the virtual exclusion of training in righteousness and Spirit-filled living. They busy themselves in their attempt to correct everyone else. Finally, there are also those pulpit ministries who have gone to seed on "instructing in righteousness." They immerse themselves in contemporary worship forms to the extent that praise often takes priority over proclamation. They speak continually about the Spirit-filled life to the virtual exclusion of teaching and preaching sound doctrine and then wonder why their churches often split and follow "every new wind of doctrine" which comes to town. The apostolic preaching model in the New Testament was one of balance. They incorporated doctrine, reproof, correction, and instruction in righteousness into their messages in a winsome, warm, and balanced manner.

A careful analysis of the Pentecostal proclamation as well as the one at Pisidian Antioch reveals that both Peter and Paul incorporated all four of these elements into the preaching experience. Simon Peter's Pentecostal proclamation recorded for all posterity in the second chapter of Acts is a perfect example. He taught doctrine. He pontificated about the doctrine of the Deity of the Lord Jesus Christ. Peter proclaimed, "God has made this Jesus, whom you crucified, both Lord and Christ" (Acts 2:36). He reproved sin in the same message when he said, "You, with the help of wicked men, put him to death by nailing him to the cross" (Acts 2:23). He corrected false paths by calling the people to change their minds and "repent" (Acts 2:38). Then he trained them in righteousness by encouraging his hearers to be baptized, to get into God's Word, to break bread together, and to grow in the grace and knowledge of our Lord Jesus Christ (Acts 2:38-46). Peter's sermon contained all four elements of an effective ministry of the Word of God. One finds the same thing in the preaching ministry of the Apostle Paul when his first recorded sermon at Antioch of Pisidia (Acts 13:13-41) is reached.

The apostolic preaching model is a balanced pattern to be emulated. Paul continued throughout his life to make emphasis of the necessity of balance in these four areas. He wrote the Book of Romans to emphasize the need of doctrine. He wrote First Corinthians to reveal the need of reproof. He wrote Galatians in an attempt to show the importance of the preacher's task of correction. He wrote Ephesians primarily to "instruct in righteousness." The faithful Bible preacher does not avoid context, confessions, controversy, or confrontation but in a balanced manner follows the apostolic pattern in preaching "doctrine, reproof, correction, and instruction in righteousness."

One of the preacher's most effective patterns is found in Paul's ministry among the Thessalonians recorded for us in Acts 17. Unlike many modern "preachers" today he did not go to Thessalonica, take several marketing surveys in an attempt to find out what the people of the city "wanted" to hear, and then develop his ministry among them in order to cater to their wants. It is said in the context of his ministry there that he and these early believers "turned their world upside down" (Acts 17:6). How did this come about? Ironically Paul did four things at Thessalonica which are in diametric opposition to the four modern principles of proclamation being espoused today. In place of avoiding context he was expository. In place of avoiding confessions he was explanatory. In place of avoiding controversy he was explicit. In place of avoiding confrontation he was expeditious. Herein lies the Biblical pattern for Bible preaching that carries with it the blessing of God which enables the church of the Lord Jesus Christ to "turn its world upside down."

While some modern preaching techniques call for the preacher to avoid context, the Apostle Paul calls for the preacher to *be expository*. When the great preacher arrived at Thessalonica, he "as was his custom, went into them, and for three Sabbaths reasoned with them from the Scriptures" (Acts 17:2). As Luke penned these words to describe the apostle's own approach to preaching, he chose a word which our English Bibles translate "reasoned." It is a compound word in Greek, the language of the New Testament. It is made up of a preposition which means "through" and a verb meaning "to speak." Paul's approach to the preaching event was to "speak through" the Scripture. He was an expository preacher! It is alarming how few in the pulpit today are reasoning ("speaking through") the Scriptures. Many reason with their hearers through current events, popular psychology, and through such things as certain habits of highly successful people. Too few Baptist pulpits "reason through the Scriptures" today in the Biblical pattern of exposition.

It is the Word of God which brings conviction. Simon Peter stood at Pentecost, took his text from Joel 2:28-32, illustrated it with Psalm 16:8-11, Psalm 68:18, and Psalm 110:1 (Acts 2:25-28, 34-35) and preached a Bible message. He established a scriptural, Biblical basis for what was happening in the manifestations of the Spirit at Pentecost and for what he desired his hearers to do in response to what they had seen and heard. Like his, our preaching should be Biblical and expository. It should be of great alarm that the Bible is so little used in the worship experience of the modern church in the western world. A preacher who does not use the Bible in his proclamation of the Gospel is akin to a surgeon going into the operating room to perform surgery on his patient without a scalpel. The preacher attempting to speak without his Bible is like a carpenter attempting to build a house without his hammer. God still speaks to us today through the prophet, Jeremiah, "Is not my word like a fire? ... and like a hammer that breaks a rock to pieces?" (Jeremiah 23:29). It is little wonder that so many churches are empty and powerless today. Relevancy has replaced the revelation of the Word in many modern pulpits.

The result of Simon Peter's Bible-based exposition at Pentecost was that his hearers "were cut to the heart" (Acts 2:37). Our English word "cut" in verse thirty-seven translates a compound Greek word made up of a preposition which means "through" and a verb which means "to pierce." Thus, their hearts were "pierced through." We have a word for this. We call it conviction and it has become one of the lost words in our Christian vocabulary. When the men and women at Pentecost heard Peter's Gospel message and realized they were personally responsible for the crucifixion of the Lord Jesus, their hearts were broken and they began to ask, "What shall we do?" (Acts 2:37). Why aren't more people's hearts cut in our churches today? It is because they do not realize they must take personal responsibility for their sin. Why are they ignorant of this fact? Many of them have never heard a preacher "speak through" the Scriptures and allow the Word of God to bring conviction. Thus by not being expository in their approach they are no longer personal in their application. Biblical, expository preaching is what the Holy Spirit uses to bring about conviction of sin. God said that His Word "will not return to me empty, but will accomplish what I desire and achieve the purpose for which I sent it" (Isaiah 55:11).

Too many sermons today are preached only in first person plural ("we") or in third person plural ("they"). This has been the emphasis of much of the teaching related to preaching in the last generation. There has been a definite move away from second person singular ("you") in the preaching event. A careful observation of the apostolic preaching model in Acts will reveal that these early and anointed preachers preached often in second person so as to call upon their hearers to take personal responsibility for their own sin in order to find the freedom which issues from genuine repentance and forgiveness of sins. Listen to Simon Peter as he preached at Pentecost, "Jesus of Nazareth was a man accredited by God to *you* through him, as *you* yourselves know. This man was handed over to *you* by God's set purpose and foreknowledge; and *you*, with the help of wicked men, put him to death" (Acts 2:22-23; emphasis added).

Many preachers today are afraid of offending modern mind-sets, deacons, elders, large givers, civic leaders, politicians, and various others. Their preaching avoids confrontation with others and personal responsibility for personal sin. Thus, their proclamation is not personal. It is indirect and nonconfrontational. It does not bring about true conviction of sin nor does it point men and women to their need of a personal Savior. Charles Finney said, "Preaching should be direct. The Gospel should be preached to men, and not about men. The minister must address his hearers. He must preach to them about themselves, and not leave the impression that he is preaching to them about others."[2] Simon Peter preached, "You, You, You!" He was confrontational and challenging to his hearers. And the result? "When the people heard this, they were cut to the heart" (Acts 2:37). God used Peter's expository proclamation to prick the hearts of the hearers with conviction of sin.

Conviction always precedes conversion. My first pastorate was in Hobart, Oklahoma. It was there on the plains of Southwestern Oklahoma in the midst of those good and godly wheat farmers where I began to beat out on the anvil of personal experience the preaching event. I learned from those dear old men who had spent a lifetime in two places, their fields and their Bibles. They taught me that there were several things necessary in order to grow a good crop. First, the ground had to be broken. They would ride their tractors plowing up and down the fields turning the sod over and over, breaking up the hardened earth. Next, the seed had to be planted. Then the wheat was cultivated, watered, and nurtured. Finally, around the first of June every year, the harvest was gathered.

Many churches today wonder why they never reap a harvest. Perhaps they have not broken the ground in a long time. It is the Word of God that cuts the human heart. Our preaching must so "reason through the Scripture" that it becomes to our heart like the plow that breaks open the hardened earth. We will never see the harvest without the preaching of the Word of God.

The preacher's job description has not changed through the centuries. Our task is to "speak through the Scriptures" as Paul did in Thessalonica and as Peter did at Pentecost. In a day when many are encouraging young preachers to avoid context, Paul's words come echoing down through the corridors of the centuries, "Be expository! Reason with your hearers, speak through the Scriptures."

While some modern preaching techniques call upon the preacher in our contemporary culture to avoid confessions, the Apostle Paul calls for the preacher to *be explanatory*. Luke, the writer of Acts, tells us that Paul not only reasoned with his hearers from the Scriptures, but he was also "explaining" the Word to them (Acts 17:3). The word we translate "explaining" in our English Bibles is from a Greek word which comes once again from the preposition meaning "through" and a verb which means "to open." Thus we see that for Paul, Gospel preaching was not simply "speaking through the Scriptures" in an expository fashion but also entailed the "opening through of the Scriptures" in an explanatory way. This same Greek word is used in other places in the New Testament to describe the opening of the womb or the opening of the door. It also appears in Luke 24:32 to describe how the Emmaus disciples' hearts began to burn within them as the risen Lord Jesus began to "open the Scripture" to them. This is the preacher's task, to speak through and open through the Scripture for the hearers.

Here at Thessalonica Paul was "explaining" the Gospel, the death, burial and resurrection of the Lord Jesus Christ. He "reasoned with them from the Scriptures, explaining and demonstrating that the Christ had to suffer and rise again from the dead, and saying, 'This Jesus whom I preach to you is the Christ.'" (Acts 17:2-3). There is no Biblical preaching without the Gospel, the good news of the death, burial and resurrection of our Lord. Paul "explained" this to his hearers. Paul had two themes in his preaching at Thessalonica, the cross and the resurrection. He was an astute theologian, but he never preached theology. He used theology to preach the Lord Jesus. At the heart of our message is that Christ "had to suffer" and that, as the apostle states, He is "the one and only Christ" (definite article in Greek). There is no other savior, no other way to the Father.

When Paul preached, he "opened through the word" to his hearers. He was explanatory. This is our job, whether it is in the pulpit, in the classroom, across the counseling table or wherever. And, parenthetically it is a very difficult task to do so without a working knowledge of the language of the New Testament. Does it make sense that the preacher whose task it is to "speak through and open through the Scripture" has at his disposal the language in which his Bible was written and is not willing to pay the price of study in order to know it?

In a day of superficiality when modern preaching techniques are calling upon the preacher to avoid context and confessions of doctrinal truth, Paul's words are poignant, pertinent, and practical. He is still calling upon us to be expository and to be explanatory, to open up doctrinal truth to our hearers and to preach that Jesus is "the" Christ.

While some modern preaching techniques call upon the preacher in our social society to avoid controversy, Paul calls upon the preacher of the Gospel to *be explicit*. Luke continues his account of Paul's own preaching style by saying he not only was "reasoning" and explaining" but also "demonstrating" the Scriptures to his hearers (Acts 17:3). In the language of the New Testament Paul chooses a Greek word which we translate "demonstrating" in our English Bibles. That comes from a preposition which means "beside" and a verb which means "to lay or to lie down." Hence the word literally means "to lie down alongside." It is used in legal terms to describe one who gives evidence, who "lays alongside" the facts certain evidence to support his or her case. Paul is admonishing the preacher here to not be afraid of "laying it out," to speak the truth in love even if it is offensive and controversial. In the context of Acts 17:1-4 Paul is "demonstrating," laying out the evidence that Jesus is, indeed, the Christ and that He did indeed rise from the dead. He presents evidence to back up the fulfilled prophecies of Isaiah 53, Psalm 22, and Psalm 69 as well as the various Old Testament shadows and types of the coming Christ. He was explicit in his approach.

The preacher of the Gospel message should "lay out alongside" the facts of the Gospel his life which "demonstrates" the validity of the message. Our lives should certainly be evidence of the validity of what we preach and proclaim. Paul "laid it out." He presented the evidence. That is the preacher's task. This entails a systematic theology and a knowledge of Bible doctrine as well as a life which matches our lips.

In a day when many are shying away from any and all types of controversial subjects from the pulpit, the apostle's words ring loud and clear. He is saying to every preacher today in this millennium, "Be explicit, tell it like it is, lay it out and with holy boldness speak the truth to contemporary culture and speak it in love."

While some are advocating the preacher should avoid context, avoid confessions, and avoid controversies, others are warning to also avoid confrontation. To this Paul states flatly, *be_expeditious* in your approach to preaching the Gospel. The Bible records that he "went in to them ... and some of them were persuaded; and ... joined Paul and Silas" (Acts 17:2,4). The great apostle began with the end in mind. He was possessed with the Gospel message and had a sense of urgency. He "went in to them" at Thessalonica, "persuaded" them, and they "joined" him in the faith.

The preacher's task is to "persuade" his hearers. This English word translates a Greek word, which means to induce one by words to believe. It carried with it the connotation of yielding to or complying with a certain persuasion.

Paul did not shy away from bringing his hearers into a confrontation with the Lord Jesus himself. Paul gave an appeal. He was winsome and persuasive in his preaching and the result was that many "joined" him (Acts 17:4). Our English word "joined" translates a Greek word, which comes from a preposition meaning "with, unto or among" and a verb meaning "to obtain an inheritance." These Thessalonians heard the Gospel preaching of Paul and made a conscious decision to take as their very own private possession the Lord Jesus Christ. Paul "persuaded" them and they "joined" him in the faith. This is still happening today wherever the Bible is preached and the preacher is expository, explanatory, explicit and expeditious.

All through the New Testament we find this pattern for Biblical proclamation. Recorded in Acts chapter eleven in connection with the great missionary church in Antioch is another poignant apostolic pattern of Biblical preaching. In describing the Bible preaching ministry in Antioch by those of the diaspora following the stoning of Stephen as well as that of such well known first century preachers as Barnabas and Paul three very important words are found. They "preached" (Acts 11:20) the Word at Antioch. The Greek word here is a familiar one which carries with it a note of pathos and passion as they preached and called for evangelistic decisions. We also read in the context a word which describes the way they used the preaching of the Word to encourage and exhort the believers in Antioch. But this was not all. They also "taught" a great number of people from the Word of God.

We continually see evidenced throughout the early church a balanced ministry of the Word of God. Some churches seldom encourage or teach the Word but are tenacious in their attempts to "evangelize." To become out of balance in the preaching ministry can mean that we may become overly confrontational in our approach to the preaching of the Gospel. On the other hand, those who "teach" to the virtual exclusion of evangelism and encouragement may have a tendency to become overly confessional. Throughout the decades of the twentieth century Baptists have enjoyed the supernatural blessing of God upon their congregations because, by and large, they have maintained a balanced and Biblical approach to the task of preaching the Gospel. They are known for their evangelistic zeal and passion as well as their ministry of encouragement and their strong emphasis upon the teaching of Bible doctrine.

Engaging the culture in the twenty-first century is the church's greatest challenge. We are called upon to reach an entire generation, most of whom have never been inside a Bible preaching church nor have they sung a Christian hymn. They are characterized by a search for meaningful relationships. Many young adults in the western world have never known a meaningful relationship in life. They are homesick for a home they have never had. They also want immediate gratification and guilt-free living. The temptation for the church is to seek to build a bridge to this "lost" generation by sacrificing the revelation of the Word on the altar of relevancy. This must be avoided.

The apostles were called to reach a world more and more like our own, that is, a pagan, godless, humanistic, secular society. Recently, while visiting the reconstructed ruins of the ancient metropolis of Ephesus, I was struck by the fact that Paul entered this city with just a couple of friends and engaged its culture and transformed the entire city. How? He did not incorporate in his strategy a single element of much of the superficial church growth principles prevalent in our day. He did not engage in marketing strategies to determine what the people of Ephesus "wanted" to hear and do. He did not tailor his ministry and programs to meet the "wants" of the people of Ephesus. He preached the Word of God to them, teaching them doctrine, reproving their sin, correcting their false paths, and instructing them in righteousness. Later, from a Roman incarceration, he wrote to Timothy, a young pastor at Ephesus, and instructed him to do likewise (2 Timothy 3:16-17). When the apostle Paul concluded his own ministry in this great city, it is recorded by Luke as one of the most touching scenes in the Bible. They followed him down to the seaside as he boarded his ship. "He knelt down and prayed with them all. Then they all wept freely and fell on Paul's neck and kissed him, sorrowing most of all for the words which he spoke, that they would see his face no more. And they accompanied him to the ship" (Acts 20:36-38). Paul had spent his years in Ephesus building his people up in the Word of God, and his last words to them were, "So now, brethren, I commend you to God and to the Word of His grace, which is able to build you up and give you an inheritance among all those who are sanctified" (Acts 20:32).

The apostolic preaching pattern was one of explanation and application. When the preacher has concluded the preparation of his sermon, he should ask himself three questions before the actual preaching event. What? So what? Now what? First, the question of "what" should be addressed. That is, what does the message say? Is it true to the text? What is the specific object? Is it clear to the hearer? Next, there is the question, "So what?" Is it relevant to the lives of men and women who are hearers? Does it meet and serve the contemporary needs of the congregation? Finally, the preacher should ask, "Now, what?" Does the sermon move the hearer to do something? Is it applicable to our daily lives? Does the hearer have a "handle" by which he or she can take the point of the sermon and put it into practice in the normal traffic patterns of his or her daily life?

It will do the preacher of the twenty-first century well to heed the words of Paul who said, Imitate me, just as I also imitate Christ" (1 Corinthians 11:1), especially when it comes to his model of Biblical preaching. Instead of avoiding context, be expository. Instead of avoiding confessions, be explanatory. Instead of avoiding controversy, be explicit. Instead of avoiding confrontation, be expeditious. It still pleases God by "the foolishness of preaching to save them that believe" (1 Corinthians 1:21).

Steven Smith

The Church's Necessity for 21st Century Survival

by Steven Smith

*T*he church bends and winds around a thousand curves intended for grace but is often stifled by extremes. Something is in vogue. Something is out of vogue. And if you are not fast enough to keep up, you are out of touch and therefore irrelevant. In a flash what was current is now ancient. There is a reason for this: the more things stay the same, the more things change.

There was a day

Imagine its 1982. A pastor gets a brochure in the mail for the latest conference. He attends the conference and likes what he hears. He is motivated to put his new found methods into practice so he goes home and has his church read about it. The method works and his friends want to know how to do it. So he calls them, on a land line phone, and tells them about it. They go to the bookstore, (It's 1982 — Amazon is only a river), and buy the book and implement it in their churches.

This is how a movement is born. People through print and telephone media propel a new thought trend that serves the body of Christ.

The situation is different today. We hear of a conference via email or social media. We decide through the immediate testimony of others if a new trend is worth imbibing or not. We text some friends, think about it and move on. If we decide to do it, all materials are delivered electronically. In fact, we may even "attend" the conference electronically.

One might observe that things have really changed. But that is not precise. The material of life has not changed, only the pace of life. Things aren't really different, but they are faster. Therefore a movement starts quicker and has a shorter life. When the movement dies, something must replace it. It makes perfect sense that trends that took dozens of years to run their course now come and go in lightening speed, with something new to replace it almost immediately. Compare the "Seeker" movement of the 80-90s to the shorter lived "Emergent" movement of the 21st century.

So, things are different. And the difference serves to show exactly how much they are the same.

People are still desperately sinful.

Life is still painful and bitter.

Marriages crumble and lives tank.

People still vainly medicate their problems away.

And technology is still the nebulous hope for those too distracted to notice that they are facilitating the same problems with updated toys; a life whose core elements have not changed. If only I had saved my eight tracks.

The people who tell you the world is different are not telling the truth or are themselves deceived. This is the same life mediated in different ways. Sin has not changed. Humanity at its core has not changed, so the need is just the same. And this is the most encouraging thing for preachers: the solution is just the same — the One who never changes, the sweet Lord Jesus.

The world is not different, it's just faster. But like the hub of a tire, the faster the tire spins the more the hub looks unchanging. Jesus is still the answer for everything. This has not changed. This will not change. The more things stay the same, the more things change.

Enter the preacher. He preaches in a world where Christ' unchanging nature stands in stark contrast to the ever increasing pace of the world around him. So how does a 21st century preacher function? There are no new revelations in what follows, but perhaps the pace of this culture makes these qualities, and our need for them, clearer, or at least more demonstrable. Below are observations about qualities the 21st century preacher must possess.

A Firm Commitment to Scripture

In a list of what an elder must be Paul tells Titus that of all things he must "hold fast the faithful treasure." The reason was that the church in Crete had young believers who needed to be encouraged and had interlopers who were trying to attack the church from within and without. Therefore Paul commanded Titus to find men who held so firmly to the word that they were "… able to give instruction in sound doctrine and also to rebuke those who contradict it."[1]

Perhaps there was a day when the preacher could reasonably assume that the people in the pew agreed with him that the leather bound book in their laps was the very word of God. Not today. The trend now is to question. If the preacher flinches when the fist of questioning is swung, he's done. He can't hesitate or balk. People will not follow a man who is uncertain.

George Whitefield's relationship with Benjamin Franklin is quite a remarkable story.[2] While Franklin never came close to confessing Christ as Whitefield preached, he loved to hear him preach and was often in attendance at his outdoor meetings. It is reported, perhaps apocryphally, that Franklin was listening to Whitefield preach when someone chided him and asked him if he really believed what he was hearing. Franklin replied, "No, but I believe he believes it". This is the idea. The culture will need to know that we believe more than ever and the 21st century Preacher must have firm conviction.

A Thoughtful Application of Scripture

Today as I write this I am sadden by the words of a thoughtless preacher. Perhaps his motivation was right, I don't know. However, the lack of love displayed and the uncaring spirit toward lost sinners seems so discordant with a Jesus who would go after sinners like a shepherd would a sheep or a father would a son.[3]

The 21st century preacher will face a multitude of challenges. He will face issues of life (genocide, infanticide, suicide); he will face issues of sexuality in ways that the former generation could not have dreamt (Gay "Marriage", the mainstreaming of sexual deviance); he will face issue of politics and education.

The way to face these issues, of course, is with a firm grasp of the Word of God while whispering to heaven for the grace of clarity and love. Truth is the only answer for this generation. But let me be clear at the risk of being misunderstood. Truth is not enough. Jesus did not stroll the Galilean hillside dropping truth bombs to let others clean up. Not at all. He actually spent time with the woman at the well—compassion unheard of in that day — before he told her, "everything she ever did."[4] He helped the woman caught in adultery.[5] He even walked into the house of a tax collector who fully demonstrated his repentance by repaying those from whom he stole.[6]

If you are reading this, I'm sure you know all this already. My point is to encourage my brothers who have a firm commitment to Scripture. Whatever happens, do not waver. Stay with the word. And while we stay with the word of Christ, stay with the method of Christ. Be as unwavering in love as you are in truth.

Perhaps one of the greatest demonstrations of compassion was the life of D.L. Moody. Moody made a commitment to share Christ at least once each day of his life. It is said of Moody that many listened to his message because they could immediately see that he genuinely loved them and wanted them to know Christ. In other words, his love made a way for the truth.

A Thorough Presentation of Scripture

It would be wonderful to know what Timothy looked like. The young pastor strapped with a very challenging ministry at a very young age. Whatever his physical appearance, I always picture I Timothy 3:10 – 4:5 like a coach talking to an athlete. Paul is intense. He has Timothy by the face mask and he is pulling him in tight. He explains that he has a trust handed down to him from generations. And now in this moment he must preach it when things are going well and preach it when they are not. He must preach in the in middle of the season and preach in the off-season. And, he must do this amid great opposition.

In the midst of this incredible challenge Paul tells Timothy to "preach the word". When I read these words I immediately think of the preacher being faithful to the full canon of Scripture before him, a canon that Timothy did not have. Timothy had the Old Testament. That fact should be considered when we read this text. Paul wrote:

> But as for you, continue in what you have learned and have firmly believed, knowing from whom you learned it and how from childhood you have been acquainted with the sacred writings, which are able to make you wise for salvation through faith in Christ Jesus. All Scripture is breathed out by God and profitable for teaching, for reproof, for correction, and for training in righteousness, that the man of God may be complete, equipped for every good work.[7]

Notice the shocking news that the OT was able to lead one to "salvation through faith in Christ Jesus." This makes me wonder if someone listening to me preach a Minor Prophet, a Psalm, or an Old Testament narrative hears Jesus. If not, while I am confessionally an inerrantist, I am not one functionally. Christ taught his disciples how all of the OT spoke of Him. The 21st century preacher will need to demonstrate to the world what was so painfully obvious to Christ.[8] We must preach Christ from the Old Testament. If we do not, we are nonverbally suggesting that the first half of the Bible is not important.

A Thoroughly Christian Presentation of Scripture.

The above sentence is oxymoronic, I get that. But what seems so strange is how many preachers of God's word want to "preach" Christ in an unchristian way. They are not preachers, they are presenters. These are not sermons they are talks. This guy is not a pastor, he is a leader, innovator, and change agent. I'm not throwing stones; really I'm not.

Regardless of whether we want the label or not, the ministry of the Gospel in many ways defines us. Certainly we have an identity outside of our calling — we are Christians, husbands, and fathers first. But while that is true, isn't it also true that we at least have an identity inside of our calling? We are preachers. Gospel preachers. That does not translate well to the world but Jesus told us to expect this. Believe it or not they actually like the fact that there is a difference between the secular and the sacred. The move to neutralize the church in its identity may have more to do with clerical insecurity than it does cultural identification.

Therefore, if God has called you to lead a church, then lead it. Sing songs that are thoroughly Christian, and preach sermons that are thoroughly Christian. You are under no obligation to apologize, in word, dress, or demeanor for what you are. You are a minister of a Christian Gospel.

A Broken Demonstration of the Gospel

The ministry is not for the faint of heart. And while it is proverbial, it is nonetheless true that every man that God uses greatly He breaks and He molds. Some have valued transparency and authenticity above the necessary clarity of Gospel presentation. That is heartbreaking. Still, the men who God uses are men who have walked dark valleys and have not done so alone. They are able to look at their people and say that they can identify with the hurts and pains because they have been there. They are there. They are shouting from the mountaintop when we are riding through the valley. And when we do it, because we must do it, it gives the people a chance to see us live the Gospel.

Our people are able to see that the God who saved us is still saving us today. He is still walking through the valley with us and encouraging us along the way. And we still preach the Gospel, with a broken heart that is being healed by the Gospel. The message is even more profound. If the preacher is not broken he will feign this. Art imitating life. The 21st century preacher will need to walk people through the Gospel, with an authenticity that tells people they can be healed from the same source that is healing him.

I remember the home I was sitting in, counseling a struggling brother. I took a call and was told that a lifelong friend had passed on to heaven. It was very expected and still hard. She lost a long battle with cancer as Jesus proclaimed his profound victory over death.

The next day I sat in the airport ready to fly out to the funeral. I scribbled these words and later read them at her funeral.

The tears and pain are the golden vein
  Through which God's mercy flows.
The yearning strain is the velvet glove
  On the hand that deals life's blows.
For every sheep needs a Shepherd
  So lonely sheep won't be alone.
As we cry tears unfettered
  For sheep who have gone home.

When I first heard the news I went back to my office to make travel plans. Standing outside my office, Gene, one of my deacons happened to be there. I explained what happened and he asked if he could pray for me. It was a simple gesture, but for Gene this was significant. I remember bowing my head just outside my office and receiving the grace of his thoughtfulness. Why that event was so significant to me I don't know. He was, in a way, explaining the Gospel back to me. My friend had passed from death to life, and that physical reality was a spiritual reality in him. It allowed the grace of Christ to be redirected back to me.

We must preach with a transparency that is very real.

A Genuine Incarnation of Scripture

What has always been true is that people need Jesus. No one is saved without hearing about Christ, so the proclamation of the Gospel is necessary. It is as true as it ever was that people need to see the preacher imbibe the Gospel that he preaches.

Our goal of course is to lead the church from the study. By this I mean that the preacher studies Scripture until he is convicted by its truth and changed by it. Then when he takes this truth to the pulpit it is evident to all that there has been a very real, yet indescribable, change in the man who is preaching. Over time the people watch the man change. He makes different choices over the course of his life and the conviction that he is proclaiming becomes ever more real to him.

The people notice this and begin to imitate his life. These people are in leadership of the church and the church begins to change. The change that takes place started with a willingness to allow the Holy Spirit of Jesus Christ to convict the man in his private time with Christ in His Word. This process is slow and often invisible, but it happens to the one with a willing heart.

Without this change, the sermons still go on. They might even be "good" in some way. However, what they will lack is the ability to effect long term change. The proclamation of the Gospel without the imitation of the Gospel is temporary. Proclamation with imitation is life.

And that brings us to Dr. Vines

I don't remember the first time I met Dr. Vines. My earliest recollection of Dr. Vines is during the midst of the Conservative Resurgence. While I don't want to make this article about that, this is the earliest context in which I met him — so the memory can't be separated from the man.

I have many memories of walking the halls of conventions during the annual meetings of the Southern Baptist Convention and meeting men like Dr. Vines. Men who appeared to be larger than life to me. I do remember all the rumblings about the sermon, "A Baptist and His Bible". I also remember the graciousness with which he, and other great men, carried themselves. Their graciousness under pressure is a remarkable trait hardly modeled today. Amazing really.

I'm among the first generation of recipients of the blessings of the Conservative Resurgence. What was/is admirable about the leaders of the movement, among so many other things, was their preaching. It is not an understatement to say that the preaching of these men was so powerful that it gave a voice to thousands of Baptists who were slowly awakening to the stench of neo-orthodoxy, and ebbing liberalism in their seminaries.

The average pew sitter understood something was wrong. The typical pastor certainly knew something was wrong when the professor that his home church sent him to study with doubted the certainty of Scripture. But like a toddler scrambling for words, they did not know how to articulate it. The leaders of the resurgence gave them a voice. A clear, articulate, eloquent voice. And so it was that when the door swung open to expose what was happening in our denomination, it swung on the hinges of preaching. In fact, it swung on a few key sermons. While the effect of these sermons is well known, perhaps it was more a consequence than by design. I'm not sure that effect could have ever been factored in.

The Presidents elected during the conservative resurgence were men who desperately loved Jesus. They sought to preach Jesus from His Word and see people saved. That motivation drove them to hone the craft of preaching. Those men, each different, worked very hard at their preaching. Perhaps none harder than Dr. Vines. That drive to exalt Christ and reach sinners with the Word sharpened a gift — the ability to preach to masses. Ultimately this gift would be used to protect a stewardship of the SBC seminaries. It was not the planning that turned the SBC, it was not the preachers, it was a love of exalting Christ from His Word. The preaching of the Bible was a consequence of a love for the Christ of the Bible. I would not want to suggest that others did not love Christ. Rather I think this is what happened: a love of the Word drove a love of preaching, which is a love of exalting Christ through His Word.

Today

The take away for the next generation, in my opinion, is not that we should attempt to preach like Dr. Vines. Rather the take away is that we should do everything we can to exalt Christ from His Word. There is a sense in which, if the attempt to return the SBC to its roots had failed, there would still be something that was gained: the great preaching that emerged during the resurgence. The take away is that we should exalt Christ from His Word and let all the rest go.

So as I think about 30 years ago I must ask myself if, in spite of all that is trending, I am faithfully exalting Christ from His word. If not, I am missing the only thing that does not change. Lord, may I see Your changeless nature and let the rest run by.

Preaching The Whole Counsel Of God

by Paige Patterson

W. A. Criswell never grew weary of reliving the answers sometimes overheard in the Crowley Building at First Baptist, Dallas to the query about when someone had affiliated with the storied congregation. "I was baptized in Leviticus" to which another would reply, "Oh, I joined in Second Corinthians." The references were to the seventeen years in which the far-famed pastor of what was then the world's largest Baptist church preached through the entire Bible "from Genesis to Maps" as Zig Ziglar used to describe it. Criswell stated the case firmly and cogently.

> There are many different kinds of preaching, but the heart of it all is to preach the Christ of the Bible, the Word of God incarnate, spoken and written. It is a strange thing that all three are called the Word of God, whether robed in flesh, or committed to a scroll in ink, or reverberating with the voice of God. The Bible and the Christ are inseparable. To minimize the written Word is to dishonor the living Word. To magnify the Book is to glorify Christ. The Bible and the Christ stand or fall together. The storm centers of Christian theology today, as in centuries past, are the deity of Christ and the infallibility of the Holy Scriptures.[1]

Jerry Vines was unable to maintain the same rate of locomotion, due in part to sharing preaching duties with Homer Lindsay for a portion of the twenty-four years during which he accomplished the same feat as Criswell. The saints of Jacksonville's First Baptist Church flocked in large numbers to hear their Georgian pastor expound every book of the Bible. The last messages delivered by Vines were from Deuteronomy, which the preacher characterized as "a book containing the five concluding sermons of Moses to the people of Israel."[2]

One obvious observation is that both pastors served long tenures. But is this desirable? Is it appropriate to preach through the Bible? Or, on the other side of the ledger, is it sinful to fail to preach through the Bible? While the last question can be answered confidently in the negative, I think it can be argued safely that every saint of God would profit rather profoundly from the opportunity across the years of his Christian pilgrimage to hear every text of the Bible explained by a faithful pastor who has studied and mastered the text of sacred literature. This chapter written in honor of Dr. Vines is designed to answer the question as to why such a practice is desirable, even to the point of becoming something of a necessity. There are three considerations. Are there significant values for the preacher? Do those values extend in some way to the church? And, finally, is there value for those who have not yet experienced the grace of God in the new birth?

Values for the Preacher

My first contention is that preaching the whole Bible provides the preacher with a host of benefits less accessible in any other approach to preaching. Most of the advantages articulated herein are based on one important assumption. Along with Criswell and Vines, this author postulates that the Bible, the Old and New Testaments, constitutes a written revelation from the eternal God. As such, this revelation was mediated through the Holy Spirit to holy men of God who were by that medium protected from all error or falsehood to which, by virtue of their humanity and the fall into sin, they would normally have been subject. As such, the Bible represents the very mind of God, not in that mind's totality, but in the portion of His mind that He chose to reveal to us for our salvation, sanctification, and edification.

The Preacher Learns the Scriptures

By preaching through the whole Bible, the preacher *learns the Scriptures* in a way that transcends any other method. What is preached or taught must necessarily be mastered to a greater degree than that which is merely read or studied. Anyone involved in a public speaking activity of any variety has learned that truth. I contend that, accentuated by the illumination of the Spirit, preaching is exponentially more enhanced by the preacher's grasp of the totality of the Bible. Charles Koller said,

> Under the burden of his message he will not think of himself as a pipe through which the truth flows out to others, but as a living embodiment of the truth to which he seeks to win others. He may not have the eloquence of a ready tongue, but will have that eloquence which is of the heart. His concern in the study will not be merely to prepare sermons, but, even more, to prepare his own heart. And when he preaches it will not be in feeble whispers, but with the spiritual vitality of the prophets and apostles, of whom he is a lineal descendant.[3]

Vines himself made three comments concerning the effects of preaching for twenty-four years through the Scriptures. First, "My understanding of the Bible was life changing." Second, "Week by week, my studies of God's Word provided a glory hallelujah time for me." By this Vines linked his devotional walk with Christ to his study for preaching—a worthy, practical, and economic goal. Finally, he noted that "Some books were sufficiently challenging that I worked carefully through them for more than a year in advance."

Preaching Material Remains Perpetually Fresh

Small wonder that the pastor Vines *remained perpetually fresh* even to a congregation that heard him every week for twenty-four years. One can hardly anticipate a vibrant ministry of proclamation if his own heart is stale. But Vines was always learning from the text. Grappling with the meaning of the text and its applicability to his life and to the lives of his sheep made his preaching vibrant.

Vines also noted the importance of the Biblical languages for his study. His grasp of New Testament Greek is well known to any of several Biblical scholars routinely telephoned by the pastor to ask his opinion of some nuance of a particular syntactical arrangement in a text in dispute among scholars. While his Hebrew is not as developed as his Greek (he reads his Greek Testament largely without lexical aid), he learned enough and reviewed it periodically so as not only to understand the sources but also to draw significant conclusions. As he stated, "If this is really the inerrant Word of the Lord, there is just something rejuvenating about digging it out for yourself."

Harried Searching for a Topic Is Eliminated

Preaching through the Bible *eliminates the harried search for a topic*. The preacher may periodically have to decide the right timing for the next Biblical journey, but week by week his choice is pre-determined. His concentration and that of his parishioners is set. Choice of which book through which to preach is determined by the needs of the church and the prompting of the Holy Spirit. I have often suggested to my students that upon initiation of a new pastorate, 1 Corinthians almost inevitably provided an appropriate beginning. The Song of Songs and Lamentations probably should wait for a time when the congregation has been carefully nurtured.

The Pastor Becomes Ageless

In preaching through the Bible there is a sense in which *the pastor becomes ageless*. Fifteen hundred years later the homilies of Chrysostom are read with great profit. The style has altered but the message of the text is timeless, and great preachers will always be sought and studied. For example, Vines' series on Ecclesiastes is memorable and brim full of insight into the meaning of the text and simply remarkable in its application to the contemporary *sitz im leben*. Criswell's three-and-one-half-year trek through the Apocalypse may never be equaled. No one present for Vines' final sermon at Jacksonville on Deuteronomy will ever forget it.

The Pastor Prioritizes Quality Biblical Resources

Preaching through the Bible enables, no, virtually compels a pastor *to build his library resources with Biblical rather than junk resources*. The plethora of books of canned illustrations, leadership volumes, and self-help pop-psychology form the bulk of many a library. Searches for an online sermon prepared (often ineptly) by someone else produce anemic pulpits bereft of the power and presence of God. By contrast the preacher who avails himself of resources of Old Testament, New Testament, Biblical theology, history, and biography will arrive at church like a wealthy philanthropist suddenly coming to a community of poverty who themselves quickly become the recipients of his wealth. Eric W. Hayden remarked,

> A further result will be that week by week as we seek material for our introduction (authorship, etc.) we shall be driven to serious research work. The gaps in our libraries will appear as we notice our lack of commentaries on certain books, and our delving into various encyclopedias will be greatly beneficial. It will also surprise us as we read how many other texts leap up to be filed for future reference and sermon-making.[4]

The Pastor Learns to See God's Way

In the process of his labor of love, the preacher gradually learns to *see things God's way, to think God's thoughts after Him*. The problem with the human family is that "our thoughts are not God's thoughts and our ways are not His ways" (Isaiah 55:8). Tragically, a cursory exposure to much contemporary preaching will demonstrate that the pulpit scarcely exhibits the mind of God to a greater degree than does the pew. Without saturation in the Word of God how could it be otherwise? In the end, man preaches what he knows, what he believes to be important, and what has shaped his own life and thought. If he is deeply in the Word of God he will not be lured by the siren songs of lesser sources but will want nothing more than to bring the bread of God and the water of life to the spiritually famished.

The Pastor Is Recognized as a Genuine Man of God

As a direct consequence, the preacher who lives in the Word of God and preaches his walk with God will discover that his flock will come to *recognize him as a Biblical authority* and, therefore, *as a genuine man of God*. The virtues of such a development far exceed the impact of preaching and extend to his pastoral leadership of the flock of God. And even if the secular community is unable to place precisely that face on the matter, they, too, come to value the person somehow as God's man. The pastor in the Free Church tradition possesses no real power or authority. He cannot or should not force anyone to do anything. But my father often spoke of something that he called "moral ascendency." When a pastor knows God as demonstrated by his preaching of the Bible and his walk with the Lord, the people hear and often follow him simply because they know him to be a true man of God.

Values for the Congregation

If preaching the whole counsel of God, which was claimed by Paul as imminently worthy, is important for the pastor, it is crucial for the congregation. Those sheep hungry for the green pastures of God-speak, if they do not find it with their pastor will seek it elsewhere. For those who cannot yet ingest the strong meat of God's Word, these sheep are condemned to perpetual anemia, vulnerability, and spiritual weakness. Consider the advantages for the congregation who listens to a man of God proclaiming the entirety of the Biblical revelation.

God's People Will Hear from Their Pastor the Whole Counsel of God

To be certain, the Bible does not directly address mainlining drugs, in vitro fertilization, cremation, or a host of other questions. But the great principles of the Bible apply to every human circumstance. There is something, and usually there is much, in the Scriptures to prescribe how people minded after the things of God should respond to every situation. For example, the question of eating meat sacrificed to idols addressed in 1 Corinthians may seem nothing more than a historical anomaly since that precise situation is not usually a part of the culture in the West. Yet the principles enunciated by Paul in responding to the Corinthian dilemma are amazingly appropriate to almost every ethical conundrum of the present era. And the wisdom of Proverbs is ageless.

When Paul addresses the Ephesian elders on his journey to Jerusalem there are many aspects of his life and ministry that could have been the occasion for discussion. But the Apostle seems most grateful for the fact that he had not failed "to declare to you the whole counsel of God" (Acts 20:27). In fact it was on this basis that Paul could be certain that he was "innocent of the blood of all men" (Acts 20:26).

The Preacher Addresses Every Human Situation

By preaching the whole counsel of God, the *preacher addresses every human situation*. Working with students across the years, I often have to opine, "Just when you think that you have seen it all!" But while there are almost endless combinations of what is now popularly labeled "dysfunctional" human behavior, nothing is not addressed in principle in the Bible. The faithful minister of the Word of God working his way through the Bible will address each situation repeatedly. Again Hayden remarks,

> For the preacher it means that the subject is given rather than chosen. And thus in coming to certain subjects which are not our pet themes we cannot pass over them. Many preachers avoid wide areas of the Bible altogether. Many passages our forefathers gloried in expounding, we often neglect. Sometimes our texts are mere pretexts or pegs upon which we hang a few thoughts. No wonder our congregations show little interest for mid-week Bible study when their Sunday fare is so ordinary. We are thus prevented from having theological bees in the bonnet and our horizon is widened. As someone has said, "It enables a minister to preach on many a subject without causing people to ask, 'Who is he getting at?'" How many would preach on the Christian hospitality unless in going through the Bible he came to that important theme in III John 8?[5]

The Pastor Scratches Every Itch

As such, and as inelegant as it may sound, the pastor also *scratches every itch*. People may well refuse to do what God requires, but most folks have a sincere curiosity to know whether or not God has something to say. "I may proceed with divorce, but, does God have any exceptions, and if I do it anyway what will come of me?" Or "I do not want to go to war and kill someone even though I enlisted. What does God think about it?" I am amazed at how the Bible speaks to questions in my life that I was not even thinking! The Bible, faithfully read and passionately preached, finds listening ears belonging to people who think themselves to be gospel troglodytes, securely shielded in their place of hiding.

For example, Vines spoke of one of his greatest surprises. Dreading the message of the Minor Prophets, he embarked on the books out of a sense of duty. He had little enthusiasm for the task and was particularly concerned that the large middle and high school group would react negatively and head for Starbucks. "To my astonishment, they proved to be more receptive than the adults, identifying with the straight, honest talk of Joel, Amos, and others." In fact, preaching is often a humbling experience. More than a few times in my fifty-five years of preaching I have dealt with a broken and sometimes sobbing individual who through his tears spoke of something I said in my sermon that cut to his very heart. However, I had not said what he thought he heard at all. God spoke His message to the person's heart as a limited preacher faithfully expounded the Word of the Lord.

The Preacher Can Answer the Hard Questions

Preaching through the Bible enables the preacher *to answer the hard questions that we might otherwise avoid.* No one can allege that the pastor has targeted him nor his favorite act of rebellion against God. There it is in the text. The preacher comes to it, and he cannot skip it and be faithful to God. Chaste, beautiful, one man for one woman, godly intimacy—yes it is there in *Shir Hashirim*. Evil temper, anger—oh, yes, many places, but "The wrath of man works not the righteousness of God." Incest, yes. Read about Lot and his daughters and the judgment and the mercy of God.

The Congregation Becomes Biblically Literate

Preaching through the Bible *produces a Biblically literate congregation.* Of course, this is critical only if the Bible is God's Word. If it is nothing more than religious testimony, the musings of men on their spiritual experiences and their own flawed interpretations of those, then preaching through the Bible is not superior to preaching through the Jewish *Talmud*, *Pilgrim's Progress*, or Bonhoeffer's *The Cost of Discipleship*. But if God's Word matters, if what He has deemed important enough to say and have recorded matters, then nothing is as important as expounding the Bible. The undershepherd cannot be with every sheep at every moment. But he can hide God's Word in the recesses of their hearts, and it will arise like a champion to defend them wherever the predator makes his approach.

Again Vines noted that one of the effects most notable in Jacksonville's First Baptist Church was that "Many church members formerly content to occupy a pew and give a little money became Bible teachers in our Sunday Schools." It might be added that not infrequently they also became rather determined personal evangelists. And from the congregation God will call out not a few to invest themselves in the ministry of Christ as pastors and missionaries.

Almost Every Issue Will Be Addressed

A pastor cannot counsel every member about every problem. However, if he archives his sermons, *he will, over time, address almost every issue and together with other godly leaders be able to provide copies of the appropriate sermon for those in need of counsel.* This has the added advantage of addressing a plethora of problems that the inquirer may never have considered.

Just recently a man, seeking an appointment to ask about a troubled marriage, approached me in a hotel lobby. I was out of the country, but someone on my staff gave him the series of sermons I had preached in chapel on the Ten Commandments. He then explained, "When I got to the last commandment, one that I never really understood, I learned what it meant to 'covet' and it healed my marriage."

The Pastor Provides an Example of Bible Study

By preaching through the Bible, the pastor *provides an example of Bible study for his congregation*, an essential discipline if they are to grow strong in the Lord and arm themselves with the whole armor of God. The pastor can urge the congregation to hear, read, study, memorize, and meditate on the Word of God, but his personal example of doing these things will do more than his exhortations. As the people observe Biblically induced holiness in their pastor, they are inevitably drawn to the well to drink for themselves.

Lives Are Changed

As the preacher preaches through the Scriptures, God's Word takes deep root in the lives of parishioners and *changed lives* become the order of the day. After Jesus "expounded in all of the Scriptures the things concerning

Himself," the Emmaus disciples reported, "did our hearts not burn within us?" (Luke 24:32). Further, they were activated, heading at once to Jerusalem to share their experience with the brethren.

Exposition of God's Word stirs the congregation to action spiritually, theologically, and morally. Jeff D. Ray said,

> But the real preaching of the real Jesus will not only have its effect on the individual but it will arouse vital reactions in society and particularly in that sphere which has come to be called "social justice." The preaching of Jesus that does not do that, and that does not seek to do that, is a stale, flat, and unprofitable travesty on Gospel preaching.[6]

Value for the Lost

Periodically, an objection is raised against preaching through the Bible. People who are lost have little interest in Biblical teaching and instruction on many topics. Therefore, is it not better to preach topical evangelistic messages or, minimally, an expository message from passages that primarily develop the nature of salvation? I am profoundly sympathetic with the evangelistic concern. Nothing is more fundamentally at stake than the eternal destinies of those outside of Christ. Years ago Clarence E. Macartney observed,

> There are, it is true, sermons for comfort and instruction, for condemnation, for special occasions. Nevertheless, the great aim and purpose of the sermon is to convert the sinner to the will of God in Christ. Our commission is still that which was given by our Lord himself to Paul: "To open their eyes, and to turn them from darkness to light, and from the power of Satan unto God, that they may receive forgiveness of sins, and inheritance among them which are sanctified by faith." Nothing less than that is the great objective of the preacher, as given to him by the Lord of Glory himself. It is this aim and purpose which makes the preacher's office the grandest upon earth and bestows upon him honors and laurels incorruptible, undefiled, and that fade not away, compared with which the laurels of a Caesar or a Napoleon are but withered weeds. That is why the true pulpit

Must stand acknowledg'd while the world shall stand,

The most important and effectual guard,

Support, and ornament of Virtue's cause.

There stands the messenger of truth: there stands

The legate of the skies—His theme divine,

His office sacred, his credentials clear.

By him the violated law speaks out

Its thunders; and by him, in strains as sweet

As angels use, the Gospel whispers peace.[7]

As important as it is to reach the lost and preach to them the everlasting Gospel, the major venue for the practice of evangelism was never the church gathered around the Word of God. At the exodus points of the parking areas, a number of churches display signs that say, "You are now entering the mission field." Evangelism is the church at work sharing its faith beyond the walls of the place of assembly. The church gathered is the church assembled to worship, to be taught, and to prepare for the missionary task. Equipped by the pastor and other teachers, the people of God enter the harvest fields to bring in the sheaves with joy.

But this should never suggest that text-driven sermons should not also be evangelistic and result in the salvation of the lost. Vines speaks of "an evangelistic twist" in every sermon. He recalls a Sunday morning at First Baptist Jacksonville, when after a message on tithing, more than sixty persons professed Christ as Savior. After describing the merits of tithing, the pastor simply concluded, "But God is not in need of your money. And until you have given yourself to Christ, the giving of material possessions would have little significance."

Every exposition properly conceived and delivered lends itself to the evangelistic task. This is neither forced nor strained but is the inevitable result of the whole message of Scripture—God's grace in pursuit of rebellious man. This is illustrated poignantly in Nehemiah 8. When Ezra and his scribes read and explained the Word of God, two things transpired. Under deep conviction, the people wept when they heard the words of the Lord. Afterword they celebrated with the rejoicing that only a cleansed heart can bring.

After all, neither a formula nor the cleverness of the preacher's appeal brings men to Christ and effects salvation. In my own years in the pastorate, I discovered that just as many lost people came to Christ when I was preaching essentially to the saints as when I was preaching an overtly evangelistic message. The preacher who fails to trust the power of the Word of God under the influence of the Spirit of God to change men's lives makes a tragic error. The author of Hebrews said it right when he noted that, "The Word of God is living and powerful, and sharper than any two-edged sword, piercing even to the division of soul and spirit, and of joints and marrow, and is a discerner of the thoughts and intents of the heart" (Hebrews 4:12).

Conclusion

In conclusion, I intend no unkindness when observing that the highest calling is the opportunity to proclaim, explain, and apply the Word of God to all who will hear. To do less, in the end, is an exercise of human pride, deluding the preacher into believing that his own thoughts and expressions are of greater significance than the Word of God. To fail to preach what God has said is to fail as a shepherd of the flock. If that conclusion is granted, then to follow the example of pastors like Jerry Vines and proclaim the whole of the Biblical text has yet to be more salubrious and pleasing to God. Preach the whole Bible!

In the superb manual on preaching written by Jerry Vines and Jim Shaddix, Vines provides this testimony.

> My efforts at the beginning were poor and tentative. As I went along, however, I began to notice a change in my ministry. The people started bringing their Bibles; they showed more interest. I saw growth in the spiritual lives of my people. That convinced me of the value of expository preaching. The value to my own life is beyond my ability to place on the printed page. Only eternity will reveal what the expository method of preaching has done for me. The value in the lives of the people who have heard me preach will await the evaluation of the judgment seat of Christ. But there is little doubt in my mind that the people themselves have been blessed through the preaching of expository sermons.[8]

This testimony of Jerry Vines ought to be the witness of every preacher in America. If it were, the nation would find itself in the grasp of a heaven-sent revival. Or as W. A. Criswell described his experience:

> A remarkable thing happens when a pastor preaches through a book of the Bible. Too many preachers walk up and down their studies wringing their hands, crying: "What shall I preach? And where can I get the pertinent material I need for my listening saints?"
>
> I also walk up and down my study, but my cry is altogether different. There is so much to preach, and so much God has said that I am afraid I am going to die before I have delivered the messages that I see in God's Book. Those two attitudes are as different as up and down and light and dark. When the preacher is expounding a Bible book, his text is automatically stated. All he need do is find out what the text says and what it means to us today.[9]

Measuring Success in Biblical Preaching

by Stephen Rummage

*I*n the spring of 1991, I enrolled at seminary. The limits of my knowledge as I walked on campus for the first time were truly astounding.

I knew as much Bible as any typical Baptist boy who had gone to Sunday school and preaching services all his life would know. I also knew how to get from my dorm room to the chapel and to the library. And, I knew a little about how to read, write, and study. Beyond that, I didn't know much at all. I'm not sure if I had ever heard the term *expository preaching*. I'm certain that I had heard only a few expository sermons. But, I knew I was called by God to preach. And I knew that, the Lord being my helper, I wanted to learn to preach well.

The first seminary class I attended was a sermon preparation course. At the beginning of his first lecture, our professor told the class he was going to teach us to preach messages that came directly out of the Bible, so we could preach without notes, and so people who listened would want to take notes. While I wondered if I could ever preach the way he was describing, I was still thrilled at the prospect.

As we walked out after the lecture that day, an excited classmate said to me, "Rummage, I think our prof's going to teach us to preach the way Dr. Vines preaches."

I asked, "Who is Dr. Vines?"

My new friend looked at me as if I must have just arrived on the planet, "He's only the greatest preacher who walks on the earth!" Then he said, "I'll get you a tape so you can hear him."

Not long after, I listened to a recording of Jerry Vines preaching. I had to agree with my friend. I had never heard anyone preach like this. The message was straight from the Bible, and delivered with incredible passion and power. As he preached, Dr. Vines explained the meaning of the Biblical text and showed how it applied to life. His points were clear and memorable. I listened, laughed, wept, wrote down key thoughts I wanted to remember, and asked God to help me adjust my life to the convicting truths of his sermon.

After my initial time hearing Dr. Vines preach, I played that tape over and over again. By then, I was listening not just to the spiritual and Biblical truths Dr. Vines was proclaiming, I was listening to learn *how* he proclaimed them so effectively, how he structured his message, and how he explained, illustrated, and applied the Biblical text. Soon thereafter, a friend let me know that Dr. Vines had written two books on preaching, one on sermon prep and another on delivery. I immediately bought both books and devoured them. As I read, my goal was simple: to learn to preach with effectiveness and success. *Maybe one day,* I thought, *I could preach a little like Dr. Vines does.*

Since then, I've read scores of other books on preaching, but few have influenced me as profoundly as *A Practical Guide to Sermon Preparation* and *A Guide to Effective Sermon Delivery*.[1] To a large degree, my understanding of what makes a sermon successful was shaped by Dr. Vines's own preaching philosophy. With that in mind, I suggest eight questions for my preacher brothers to ask to determine whether our preaching is successful, based on principles found in the writings of Jerry Vines.

Is the sermon expositional?

Dr. Vines has written that his life and ministry were changed when he decided to devote himself to expository preaching,[2] and his testimony could be repeated by countless other preachers who have devoted themselves to exposition. To understand the nature of the expository sermon, I would suggest avoiding definitions that focus on length of Biblical text or a particular outlining style. Instead, the core of an expository sermon is its goal. An expository sermon is one in which the message's subject and structure seek to reflect the subject and structure of a given passage of Scripture. The preacher is attempting to say the same thing in his message that the Biblical text is saying.

A hallmark of Dr. Vines's homiletical theory and practice is his commitment to expository preaching not merely as a style of preaching among other styles, but as the unequivocally best method.[3] He identifies the following qualities of an expository sermon: (1) It must be based upon a passage from the Bible. (2) The actual meaning of the Bible passage must be found. (3) The meaning must be related to the passage's context. (4) The eternal truths in the passage must be made clear. (5) Those truths must be gathered around a compelling theme. (6) The main points of the sermon must be drawn from the Scripture verses themselves. (7) Every method to apply the truths found in the verse must be utilized. (8) The hearers must be called to live out these truths in daily life.[4]

The Bible passage under consideration may be longer or shorter, provided that the passage is a complete unit of meaning. The message may have a structured outline, or a more freeform organization. Whatever the length of the sermon text or method of outlining, an expository sermon puts the meaning of a passage on display, opening up a portion of Scripture to the listeners and allowing them to see its substance. In this regard, no sermon is successfully Biblical unless it is expositional.

Is the individual sermon part of a larger plan to teach the Scripture systematically?

As Paul bade farewell to the Ephesian elders, he said, "I testify to you this day that I am innocent of the blood of all men. For I have not shunned to declare to you the whole counsel of God" (Acts 20:26-27). To "shun" means to shrink or draw back. Left to our own designs, preachers are apt either consciously or unwittingly to avoid preaching certain aspects of the "whole counsel of God." Some Bible truths wind up being neglected because they are controversial or sensitive. Other aspects of God's truth are left unpreached because the preacher simply is not aware of them or doesn't remember to address them.

Preaching expository series through Bible books ensures that a pastor teaches his church the whole counsel of God's Word. Dr. Vines advocates an expository plan of preaching as the preferred way to teach a congregation the Scriptures, writing, "The best preaching a man can do is to go through the books of the Bible, book by book, paragraph by paragraph, in a systematic fashion. ... There is no better way to convey the truths of God's Word."[5]

While an expository sermon is a single message that exposes the meaning of a passage, the expository series is a plan that allows the preacher to preach systematically through a book of the Bible or a section of a book. The expository series honors the continuity of the Biblical text. Rather than the preacher jumping from one passage to another with each successive week, the Biblical text itself is determining which subjects are addressed from the pulpit.

Does the sermon have a clear central idea?

A charge sometimes laid against expository preaching is that it is nothing more than a shapeless commentary on Scripture, with no compelling theme. Instead of being a focused message, it is said, the expository sermon presents only a detailed, sometimes laborious analysis of the minute details of the Bible text. Dr. Vines counters that the best type of expository preaching is "built around a central theme."[6]

From a rhetorical standpoint, it is always wise for a speaker to have one main thought he is communicating. Without a strong main idea, a message becomes too diffused to be effective. A sermon about ten things is a sermon about nothing. However, the rationale for having a clear central idea goes far deeper. An expositor must have a clear central idea in order to honor the Bible passage he is preaching. Every passage of Scripture has a central subject, a main idea that the Biblical author is presenting. Faithful interpretation of any passage of Scripture requires discovering the Biblical author's central idea. The expository preacher's task is to find the subject of the Biblical text and then communicate that main idea in his sermon.

Articulating the main idea of the message can be the hardest aspect of preaching a sermon. Though the central idea is only one sentence, it may take hours of labor to find the right words for that sentence. However, the value of having a clearly stated main idea makes the effort worthwhile. The main idea is the core of the preacher's message. No preacher is ready to preach until he can state the essence of the message in one simple sentence. Likewise, no sermon is successful if the listener has not heard and understood the central idea.

Is the sermon organized effectively?

In addition to having a clear central idea, a successful expository sermon will have a structure that is easy for the listener to follow. Dr. Vines considers the outline the most important part of sermon organization,[7] advocating a sermon structure that flows logically from the text: "In expository sermon preparation the main points should be drawn from the passage. This is one of the distinguishing characteristics of expository sermons. An outline is not imposed upon the Scripture passage. Rather, the outline naturally emerges from the material of the passage at hand."[8]

I have observed three major weaknesses in expository sermon outlines. One weakness is when the outline is overly complicated by subpoints. While subpoints look neat and orderly on paper, few preachers can communicate with enough oral clarity for the listener to distinguish between major points and subpoints when the message is actually being delivered. Avoiding subpoints unless they are demanded by the text will usually make a sermon outline more effective.

Another weakness is when the preacher strains to make his outline alliterated. I am not saying that alliteration should be avoided altogether.[9] However, the preacher's primary concerns in formulating his outline points should be clarity and precision rather than alliteration. If the words we use to alliterate our messages are obscure and hard to understand or if they don't quite communicate the idea of the text accurately, it would be better to omit alliteration.

A third weakness is when the sermon points stray from the main idea of the message. When this happens, each point begins to seem like a small sermon of its own rather than being part of a cohesive whole. Here's a good rule of thumb for your outline: Every point in an expository sermon should *point back* to the main idea. This will happen readily if the expository preacher's main idea is indeed the central thought of the Bible passage and if the outline follows the structure of the text.

Does the sermon aim at transformation?

For preaching to be authentically Biblical, a sermon must call for transformation through faith and obedience. According to 2 Timothy 4:2 preaching God's Word has three intentions: convincing, rebuking, and exhorting. To *convince* emphasizes reasoning concerning God's truth. The word *rebuke* is the same term used in Matthew 17:18, where Jesus rebuked a demonic spirit. Rebuking thus involves calling wayward spiritual forces to submit to God's will. *Exhort* is the Greek word *parakaleo*, which means to comfort and encourage. All these intentions of preaching are transformational, calling for a changed life in the listener.

The sermonic elements of explanation, illustration, and application help the preacher accomplish life transformation by speaking to different facets of the listener's personality. *Explanation* appeals to the listener's understanding. It involves telling the listener what the Biblical passage says, explaining word meanings, theological concepts, historical background, and other information connected with the text. *Illustration* aims at the listener's imagination. Material such as anecdotes, testimonies, examples, analogies, visual aids, and descriptive word pictures help the listener to see the reality of the Biblical truth being proclaimed. *Application* speaks to the listener's volition, showing the specific actions that can be taken to obey God regarding the truth of the message, and then pleading for a faith decision.

A successful sermon will have balance among these three elements. This balance is not necessarily one of time, but of attention. Dr. Vines strongly advocates this type of approach, writing, "The faithful pastor will make a serious and sincere attempt to unfold the actual grammatical, historical, contextual, and theological meaning of a passage. He will then seek to make the meaning of that passage relevant to the lives of his hearers. To do that he will properly organize, adequately illustrate, and forcibly apply its message."[10] Often, the sermonic element most associated with expository preaching is explanation of the text. When application and illustration are used properly in an expository sermon, however, they are not a departure from the exposition, but a deepening of it, moving the message from mere presentation of Biblical ideas to a call for Biblical faith and living.

Has the sermon been filtered through the preacher's heart?

A sermon has its greatest success when the Biblical message becomes a reality in the preacher's own life. Early in his sermon preparation book, Dr. Vines remarks, "The expository sermon feeds my own heart."[11] Then later, in his volume on sermon delivery, Dr. Vines uses the phrase "heart preacher," which he equates with sincerity and earnestness.[12] I believe this concept is among the most important homiletical ideas he discusses.

One of the great advantages of expository preaching is that it has the potential to change the lives not only of listeners, but also of preachers. This is because expository preachers are delivering messages that originate from God's Word rather than creating their own messages. In my own preaching experience, I have discovered that a message which originates with me (such as a topical sermon or some other type of speech) does not usually change me. However, an expository message that originates in God's Word can change my own heart I as prepare.

When a preacher prepares his message with a desire that his own heart be transformed, expository preaching becomes one of the most significant factors in a preacher's own spiritual growth. Dr. Vines observes that sermons should be born in the preacher's heart, writing "Though the preacher gets his sermon from the Bible, he must bring it to life in his heart. Though he may prepare his sermon on paper, he must deliver it from his heart."[13]

Before a sermon can be successfully delivered, you must prepare yourself even more than you prepare your message. You must allow the text you are preaching to permeate your own soul, to challenge you in your thinking, to convict you of your sin, and to encourage you in your faith. You must let the passage preach to you before you presume to preach it to your people. A message that has changed the preacher's own heart will be more passionately and sincerely delivered. Our listeners are also more likely to be convinced by the truth of our message, because they perceive that *we* are convinced.

Is the sermon delivered by a Spirit-filled preacher?

Closely related to being a heart preacher is the need to be filled with the Holy Spirit. The command to be "filled with the Spirit" in Ephesians 5:18 most certainly applies to those who are called to prepare and preach messages from God's Word. Dr. Vines identifies two major areas where the preacher must rely on the Holy Spirit: (1) for illumination as he studies, and (2) for power as he delivers the message.

Only through assistance from the Holy Spirit can a preacher understand the Bible as he prepares the message. Dr. Vines observes, "The same Holy Spirit who inspired men to write the Bible will illuminate our minds, assisting us to understand what we read."[14] Then, once the message is prepared, our preaching is only effective when it is accompanied by the Spirit's power. Dr. Vines writes, "In preaching actually two are involved, for there must be cooperation between the Spirit of God and the man of God. An awareness of this partnership brings about confidence and assurance as the preacher stands to preach."[15]

I have found that God's Spirit empowers me most in the pulpit when I am walking closely with Christ throughout the week. Certain actions and attitudes on our part invite the filling and anointing of the Spirit in our lives. If we are to be Spirit-filled preachers, we will make deliberate time for personal prayer and Bible study beyond our sermon preparation time. We will give significant parts of our day to intercessory prayer. We will confess our sins and keep our relationships right with God and others. Most importantly, we will desperately seek the Lord's hand on our lives and ministries, pleading for His anointing and power.

Is the sermon centered on the Gospel of Jesus Christ?

Successful Biblical preaching will always connect in some way to the Gospel message. This is because the supreme theme of all Scripture is redemption through Jesus Christ. Some passages are very obviously related to the Gospel. Themes such as sin, grace, mercy, forgiveness, eternal life, or salvation are dominant in the text. In those cases, simply preaching the words of the text will lead to proclamation of the Gospel. At other times, the dominant themes in the text under consideration may be related to ethics, morality, the family, giving, or some other subject. Even so, there is always a subtext of redemption in any Scripture passage. Faithful Bible preaching requires showing our listeners how the message we are preaching connects with Jesus.

Even passages that seem lackluster or disconnected from real life take on a new excitement when we seek to preach Christ from those texts. Dr. Vines observes, "Suddenly the Lord Jesus Christ appears in the passage. Having found Him we discover a treasure chest of riches. On the Lord's day, as we preach Jesus from that passage, the whole congregation will be greatly enriched."[16]

An expository sermon that is not intensely shaped by the good news of Christ will tend to become a moral lesson, a grammar lesson, a theology lesson, or a history lesson. When the message is saturated by the Gospel, however, the message will offer real hope to the listener and will call the listener to faith. Consequently, the sermon can more authentically be directed toward an evangelistic appeal at the appropriate time in the preaching event, because the Gospel has been an integral part of the entire message.

Conclusion

Near the end of *A Practical Guide to Sermon Preparation*, Dr. Vines writes, "Preparing effective expository sermons can be a most frustrating work. Weekly my own heart is overwhelmed by a sense of inadequacy. Who among us can do justice to our responsibility to preach what God says in His Word? But God has chosen in the past, and still chooses today to use weak, inadequate human vessels to communicate His living Word to men."[17]

Most preachers have experienced the same sense of insufficiency Dr. Vines described, as well as the awareness of our absolute dependence on God as we preach. We understand that our success is not measured by any accolades we might get from others, but by how closely our preaching conforms to healthy principles for Biblical preaching. Preaching God's Word would be audacious and presumptuous were it not for the fact that God has commanded it, and He has called and gifted preachers to fulfill that command. God's calling on the preacher's life requires our absolute best when we stand to preach. We seek success in the pulpit not for the sake of our accomplishment, but for the glory of the Lord who has called us.

A Theology of Expository Preaching

by Steve Lemke

The theology of expository preaching is a topic that is sometimes assumed or overlooked, and yet is crucially important. Sound preaching should reflect sound theology (Titus 1:9-16; 1 Timothy 4:6-7, 13-16; 2 Timothy 2:15; 3:14-17; 4:2). Faithful preachers must handle the Word of God with integrity (2 Corinthians 4:2). Scripture repeats numerous warnings about the dire consequences of ministers who teach false doctrine (James 3:1; 1 Timothy 4:1-16, 6:1-4; 2 Timothy 2:15-19; 3:13; 4:3-4; 2 Peter 2:1-22). Not only should sermons reflect sound theology, but the practice of preaching itself should be grounded in a sound theology of preaching. This article will propose just such a theological foundation for expository preaching, reflecting how the doctrines of Revelation, Theology, Christology, Pneumatology, Soteriology, and Ecclesiology provide a framework for Christian proclamation in general, and expository preaching in particular.

Revelation: The Doctrine of Scripture

The first question one must address in expository preaching is the source of truth and authority for preaching. Expository preaching is Word-based preaching — preaching that is based upon and derived directly from Scripture. The most fundamental theological presupposition of expository preaching is thus the Divine inspiration and authority of the Bible. The authority for expository preaching is derived from the conviction that Scripture is *theopneustos*, i.e., "God-breathed" (2 Timothy 3:16). The Bible reflects the very words of God written by the human author under the inspiration of the Holy Spirit. As Peter described this process, "holy men of God spoke as they were moved by the Holy Spirit" (2 Peter 1:21). If Scripture is not Divinely inspired, there is no real authority in Scripture for preaching. A Bible that is just a compilation of human ideas and wisdom has little authority and offers little help. Only a Divinely inspired Scripture provides an authoritative basis for preaching. The Bible is not just a collection of good ideas or lofty human thoughts; it is the Word of God. In Jesus' parable of the sower and the seeds, the seed being sown is the Word of God (Mark 4:14). Paul instructed the young minister Timothy to "preach the Word" (2 Timothy 4:2-5), and to read and exposit Scripture in teaching sound doctrine (1 Timothy 4:11-16).

In his famous sermon at the 1987 Southern Baptist Convention Pastor's Conference, "A Baptist and His Bible," Dr. Vines drew careful attention to the phrase "holy Scriptures" in 2 Timothy 3:15. Vines noted that the word *gramata* is used here, to designate "the writings or the documents," in distinction from *graphe* in the next verse, 2 Timothy 3:16, or *logos* in 2 Corinthians 4:2. But Vines drew special attention to the word *hiera*, translated "holy" in this verse, which was used instead of the more usual word *hagios*. Vines noted that 1 Corinthians 9:13 is the only other significant place in the New Testament that *hiera* is used, describing the sacred things in the temple. By applying this word, Paul wanted to "emphasize the special reverence attached to this book" to his young minister friend Timothy. Thus should every preacher approach Scripture – with a sense of awe and reverence.[1]

The particular view of the inspiration of Scripture being described here is normally called the *plenary verbal* view of inspiration. To be "verbal" inspiration means that God's inspiration extends not just to general concepts and ideas, but to the very words of Scripture. To be "*plenary* verbal" means that inspiration is *fully* verbal, extending God's inspiration to each and every word. The Holy Spirit so superintended the process of inspiration that every word accurately reflects the Word of God, even though it is within the vocabulary and worldview of the human author. If a preacher does not believe in plenary verbal inspiration, then Scripture might be understood to communicate merely broad, general ideas about God. In this perspective, each word may or may not actually communicate the Word of God, and thus one could not have absolute confidence in the truth of every statement in Scripture. No particular weight could be assigned to the tense, declension, or voice of a word. However, if each word is Divinely inspired, the grammatical details of the word matter. The interpretation of a text and the basis of a point in a sermon might depend upon the tense or some other grammatical detail. Expository preaching presupposes that every word in Scripture is inspired by God, and thus important insights may depend upon the specific meaning of a word as determined by its lexical meaning (taking into account its normal range of meanings according to its tense, declension, or voice).

The inerrancy of Scripture is also foundational for expository preaching. If Scripture is not true, the basis for expositional preaching is merely shifting sand, an unworthy foundation for life. However, if the Word of God is the bedrock of truth, it gives authority and credibility to expository preaching (Matthew 7:24-29). God's Word when faithfully proclaimed will not return void, but will accomplish God's purpose effectively (Isaiah 55:11).

A commitment to the Divine inspiration and inerrancy of the Bible demands that the expositor practice good hermeneutics. It is incumbent upon the faithful expositor who believes that each word of Scripture is Divinely inspired not to handle the Word of God "deceitfully" (2 Corinthians 4:2), but to rightly divide the Word of truth (2 Timothy 2:15). As Vines and Shaddix express it,

> Careful exegesis leads the expositor to good hermeneutics — the science of interpreting what a passage of Scripture means. The Greek word translated hermeneutics is *hermēneuō* ... [which often] means to translate. A related word, *diērmeneuō*, means to expound or to interpret. Hermeneutics enables the preacher to determine what a text *means* as opposed to just what it *says*.[2]

Utilizing sound hermeneutics, the preacher exegetes the Scripture verse by verse, seeking the true meaning of the text. Exegesis is "the procedure one follows for the discovering the Holy Spirit's intent" in a text of Scripture.[3] When the preacher is confident of the meaning of the text, the next step is to "expose" this Biblical truth to the congregation through the sermon.

Vines and Shaddix define "exposition" as "the process of laying open a Biblical text in such a way that its original meaning is brought to bear on the lives of contemporary listeners."[4] God will bless the ministry of the preacher who faithfully proclaims the Word of God week by week, who exegetes the Scripture with sound hermeneutics, and who with the guidance of the Holy Spirit exposits those truths with clarity to the lives of the congregation.[5]

Perhaps some might think that such an assertion about Biblical inerrancy and authority is unnecessary. Didn't the conservatives win the "Battle for the Bible" in the SBC? The answer is "yes" and "no." Yes, we did win the battle of the Bible in the SBC in the 1980s. Conservative Baptists fought against the errors of higher critical methodology, humanistic views of inspiration, and neo-orthodox theology.[6] Unfortunately, that battle was over three decades ago. A new generation of ministers has arisen who were infants or not yet born during the Conservative Resurgence in the Southern Baptist Convention. They know little about what the denominational controversy was all about, and they have little interest in it. One student recently described inerrancy as "an old man's battle." The saying is true as ever: "Those who will not learn from history are doomed to repeat it."[7] Eternal vigilance is required to maintain doctrinal purity. As G. K. Chesterton famously said, "To keep a white fence looking white, you can't just leave it as it is. You have to keep repainting it white over and over again to keep it looking the same."[8] If we are going to keep Southern Baptists believing that the Bible is the inerrant, infallible Word of God, we're going to have to keep repainting that fence in every generation. We need not only to hold to scriptural authority in our hearts, but to teach it diligently to the next generation over and over again (cp. Deuteronomy 6:4-9).

We may be entering an era in which there is a dearth of the preaching and hearing of the Word of God (Amos 8:9-11, Romans 10:17). As Danny Akin has said so aptly,

> Seduced by the sirens of modernity, we have jettisoned a Word-based ministry that is expository in nature. We have in our attempt to be popular and relevant become foolish and irrelevant. Skiing across the surface needs of a fallen sinful humanity, we have turned the pulpit into a pop psychology side show and a feel-good pit stop ...

Preaching the cross of Christ and the bloody atonement accomplished by His death is the exception, not the norm."[9]

One would not expect a similar assessment of the state of conservative evangelical Christian preaching from a mainline liberal Protestant such as William Willimon, Dean of the Chapel at Duke University. However, in an article entitled "Been There, Preached That: Today's Conservatives Sound Like Yesterday's Liberals," Willimon laments that Baptists and other evangelicals have abandoned Biblical preaching:

> I'm a mainline-liberal Protestant-Methodist-type Christian. I know we're soft on Scripture. . . . I know we play fast and loose with Scripture. But I've always had this fantasy that somewhere, like in Texas, there were preachers who preached it all, Genesis to Revelation, without blinking an eye, straight from the Scofield Chain Reference – just like Jesus said it. I took great comfort in knowing that, even while I preached a pitifully compromised, "Pealed"-down gospel, that somewhere, good old Bible-believing preachers were offering their congregations the unadulterated Word, straight up. Do you know how disillusioning it has been for me to realize that many of these self-proclaimed Biblical preachers now sound more like liberal mainliners than liberal mainliners?" At the very time those of us in the mainline, old-line, sidelined were repenting of our pop psychological pap and rediscovering the joy of disciplined Biblical preaching , these "Biblical preachers" were becoming "user friendly" and "inclusive," taking their homiletical cues from the "felt needs" of us "boomers" and "busters" rather than the excruciating demands of the Bible."[10]

Willimon continues this account by recounting the story of a Baptist who called his office asking about who would be preaching at the Duke Chapel. The caller complained that his Baptist preacher was just preaching politics and social issues. He said that because he was moving through a difficult time in his life, he needed to hear a sermon about God, not about politics. Willimon concludes this story with a stunning indictment on the state of Baptist preaching today: "When you have to come to a Methodist for a Biblical sermon, that's pitiful."[11]

How sad that the conservative generation of pastors who stood firm for Biblical preaching against the liberal need-based preaching of Harry Emerson Fosdick has handed over their pulpits to a generation that imbibes of Fosdick's approach to preaching hook, line, and sinker! Fosdick taught us that our sermons should not be Biblical expositions, but should address people's felt needs and help them cope with their problems. Anyone who has confidence in God's inerrant Word knows that there is nothing more relevant to the deepest needs of the human heart than the Bible. We need to stop trying to "make the Bible relevant" and unleash the life-changing power of the Gospel. As the Apostle Paul said, "I am not ashamed of the gospel of Christ, for it is the power of God unto salvation to everyone who believes" (Romans 1:16, KJV). We need to get back to expository Gospel preaching that proclaims Jesus Christ as the Son of God who was born of a virgin, who lived a sinless life, who taught Divine truth and performed miracles, who was crucified on the cross as a substitutionary atonement for our sins, who is risen and ascended to the right hand of God to make intercession for us, and who is coming again to take us to heaven with Him. That Gospel message is what our world is hungry to hear, whether they realize it or not.

Theology: The Doctrine of God

When Divine revelation is accorded its appropriate role as the proper source for authority and truth in preaching, and good hermeneutics are applied in its interpretation, it should lead the preacher to a correct Theology (the doctrine of God). Theology is the proper object of preaching — more specifically, God as revealed in Scripture as the Trinity of God the Father, Jesus Christ the Son, and the Holy Spirit. The fundamental difference that separates preachers from other speakers is that other speakers proclaim their own ideas and the great ideas of others on a wide range of subjects, while the preacher proclaims what the Bible says about who God is and what He has done.

What does the Bible reveal about God that is foundational to proclamation? The God revealed in Scripture is a *self-revealing* God. Although there is much about God that transcends human understanding (Isaiah 55:8-9), God has revealed to us the most important aspects of His nature through Scripture and through the incarnation of His Son Jesus Christ.[12] God is personal, and He communicates with humans. He is not the distant god of

Deism, separate and transcendent from the world. In Christ, God became flesh and got His hands dirty in the world. The Word became flesh and dwelt among us (John 1:14). We need not speculate about God's character or what His will is for our lives. God has taken the initiative in revealing Himself to us and communicating who He is and what He is about in our world.

The Bible reveals that God is perfect in every way. He is all-powerful (omnipotent), all-knowing (omniscient), all-present (omnipresent), all-wise (omniscient), and all-loving (omnibenevolent).[13] He is the Creator of the universe and sustains it through His providential care. He is the sovereign Lord who reigns over all creation. No power or being can stand against His sovereign power. The Bible reveals God as expressed in the Trinity of three Persons — God the Father, God the Son, and God the Holy Spirit – "with distinct personal attributes, but without division of nature, essence, or being."[14]

What does the Bible reveal about the *character* of God? Scripture reveals that God is perfectly moral. One important aspect of His moral character that God has revealed to us is that He *is* love (1 John 4:7-8). Any depiction of God that does not characterize God as loving is unBiblical. Indeed, despite God's hatred of sin because of His holiness and righteousness, through His holy and sovereign love, the Bible makes it clear that God loves everyone in the world:[15]

> For *God so loved the world*, that He gave His only begotten Son, that whoever believes in Him shall not perish, but have eternal life. For God did not send the Son into the world to judge the world, but that the world might be saved through Him. (John 3:16-17, HSCB, italics added)[16]

> The Lord does not delay His promise, as some understand delay, but is patient with you, not wanting any to perish, but *all to come to repentance*. (2 Peter 3:9, HSCB, italics added)

> He Himself is the propitiation for our sins; and *not for ours only, but also for those of the whole world*. (1 John 2:2, HSCB, italics added)

> Beloved, let us love one another, for love is from God; and everyone who loves is born of God and knows God. The one who does

not love does not know God, for *God is love*. By this *the love of God was manifested in us*, that God has sent His only begotten Son into the world so that we might live through Him. In this is love, not that we loved God, but that *He loved us* and sent His Son to be the propitiation for our sins ... We have come to know and have believed *the love which God has for us. God is love*, and the one who abides in love abides in God, and God abides in him. (1 John 4:7-10, 16, NASB)

Scripture also describes another aspect of God's moral character — that God is holy and righteous. This aspect of God's character is expressed by His moral perfection and His commandments for us to live up to His standards (Matthew 5:48, Romans 12:2). God's holiness is also revealed in His holy wrath against all manner of sin.

Effective preaching maintains the balance of those key aspects of God's nature. Although sermons are by definition one-sided (in that they focus primarily on one teaching from one text), it is the responsibility of the preacher to balance sermons on the holiness and righteous of God with sermons on the love of God. An overly strong focus on the holiness of God presents the hearers with a God who is righteous and "wholly other" but so transcendent that He has little or no interaction with humans. An overly strong focus on the love of God, however, presents the image of a kind God who has no real objective standards. The Bible reveals that the truth about God is somewhere between these two extremes, proclaiming the love of God while upholding God's high moral standards without compromise.

Christology: The Doctrine of Christ

Jesus is the proper focus of preaching about God, for He is the Savior sent by God. A sound Christology is thus necessary for effective preaching.[17] As the *Baptist Faith and Message* words it, "All Scripture is a testimony to Christ, who is Himself the focus of Divine revelation."[18] While it is fitting for preachers to share their own experiences as illustrations, we should always heed the example of the Apostle Paul to focus our preaching on Jesus Christ, for "we preach not ourselves, but Christ Jesus the Lord" (2 Corinthians 4:5, KJV). Jesus told the devout Nicodemus, "As Moses lifted up the serpent in the wilderness, even so must the Son of Man be lifted up; so that whoever believes will in Him have eternal life" (John 3:14-15, NASB). Jesus also promised, as he entered Jerusalem to face His crucifixion, "And I, if I am lifted up from the earth, will draw all men to Myself. But He was saying this to indicate the kind of death by which He was to die" (John 12:31-32, NASB).

God sent Jesus to this world to offer salvation to all who would repent of their sins and trust Christ as their Savior. It is a repeated theme in the New Testament that Jesus' atonement is sufficient for *all* who trust in Him:

He came unto His own, and his own received Him not. But *as many as received Him*, to them gave He power to become the sons of God, *even to them that believe on His name*" (John 1:11-12, KJV, italics added).

And as Moses lifted up the serpent in the wilderness, even so must the Son of Man be lifted up, that *whoever believes in Him* should not perish but have eternal life. For *God so loved the world* that He gave His only begotten Son, that *whoever believes in Him* should not perish but have everlasting life. For God did not send His Son into the world to condemn the world, but *that the world through Him might be saved.* (John 3:14-17, NKJV, italics added)

For this is good and acceptable in the sight of God our Saviour; Who will have *all men to be saved*, and to come unto the knowledge of the truth. For there is one God, and one Mediator between God and men, the man Christ Jesus; Who *gave Himself a ransom for all*, to be testified in due time. (1 Timothy 2:3-6, KJV, italics added)

The Lord is not slack concerning His promise, as some count slackness, but is longsuffering toward us, *not willing that any should perish but that all should come to repentance.* (2 Peter 3:9, NKJV, italics added)

And he is the propitiation for our sins: and *not for ours only, but also for the sins of the whole world.* (1 John 2:2, KJV, italics added).

Paul maintained this focus on the crucifixion of Christ, by practicing Gospel-focused *kerygmatic* preaching (Gospel preaching focused on the cross of Christ). The *kerygma* is the proclamation of the essential details of the Gospel – that Jesus is the promised Messiah, the Son of God, whose coming was prophesied in the Old Testament; that His identity was confirmed by His teachings and miracles during His ministry in this world; that He was crucified and resurrected according to God's eternal plan; that He is exalted to the right hand of God; that those who repent of their sins and trust in Christ as Lord and Savior can receive forgiveness and eternal life; and that He is coming again to save His own and judge the sin of the world (Acts 2:22-39, 3:13-26, 4:10-12, 10:36-43, 13:17-41, 1 Corinthians 15:1-11).[19]

The focus of the *kerygma* is the cross of Christ. Paul told the Corinthian church that "I determined to know nothing among you except Jesus Christ and Him crucified" (1 Corinthians 2:2, HCSB). Although the Jews sought confirmation of the message by miraculous signs and Gentiles sought wisdom through philosophy, Paul asserted that "we preach Christ crucified, to Jews a stumbling block and to Gentiles foolishness, but to those who are the called, both Jews and Greeks, Christ the power of God and the wisdom of God" (1 Corinthians 1:23-24, NASB).

There is nothing wrong with preaching on subjects such as family life, Christian citizenship, moral challenges, Christian doctrine, or godly principles for living. These are important topics from the Word of God. But one's preaching ministry should always be focused on the cross of Christ, for this crucial moment in history that has the power to change lives even today.

Pneumatology: The Doctrine of the Holy Spirit

The Holy Spirit plays an indispensible and irreplaceable role in preaching.[20] A sound Pneumatology is thus a key to effective preaching because, first of all, the Holy Spirit inspired the scriptural text that is preached (2 Peter 1:21). Since He inspired the text of Scripture, the Spirit is the best source for its proper interpretation. The Spirit illumines the spiritually discerning reader of Scripture (John 16:7-14). As Vines and Shaddix put it, proper exegesis is "the procedure one follows for the discovering the Holy Spirit's intent in a Bible passage."[21]

It is also the Spirit who convicts and convinces the hearers of sermons, not the preacher. Jesus said that the Spirit "will convict the world of sin, righteousness, and judgment" (John 16:8, HCSB). Persons are not saved by mere human words, but by the conviction and prompting of the Holy Spirit.[22] The *Baptist Faith and Message 2000* highlights the crucial role that the Holy Spirit plays in conversion, sanctification, and Christian service:

> [The Holy Spirit] convicts men of sin, of righteousness, and of judgment. He calls men to the Saviour, and effects regeneration. At the moment of regeneration He baptizes every believer into the Body of Christ. He cultivates Christian character, comforts believers, and bestows the spiritual gifts by which they serve God through His church. He seals the believer unto the day of final redemption. His presence in the Christian is the guarantee that God will bring the believer into the fullness of the stature of Christ. He enlightens and empowers the believer and the church in worship, evangelism, and service.[23]

Only the minister who preaches in the power of the Spirit will have the life-changing results that only the Spirit can work in someone's life. Wise preachers realize that dependence upon the Holy Spirit is an essential for effective preaching. A preacher can have a a great sermon outline, skillful exposition, apt illustrations, a well-designed set of presentation program slides on the screen to underscore the main points of the sermon, an excellent voice, and well-orchestrated gestures, but without the unction of the Holy Spirit, the preacher is like a sounding brass or clanging cymbal, because the sermon alone lacks the power to convict hearers and bring life transformation. Without the anointing of the Spirit, even the best-crafted sermon can become merely a dry lecture. With the anointing of the Spirit, even an imperfect message can be used mightily by God to transform lives.

Soteriology: The Doctrine of Salvation

The good news of salvation through Jesus Christ is so surprising that it is a stumbling block or foolishness from the perspective of the world (1 Corinthians 1:18-25, 2 Corinthians 4:1-6). The word translated "stumbling block" in 1 Corinthians 1: 23 is *skandalon*, from which we get the English word "scandal." The world sought salvation by intellectual enlightenment and human good works, but God provided salvation as a gift of grace through the atoning sacrifice of Christ on the cross.

Not only is the message of the Gospel surprising and scandalous, but Scripture ties salvation closely to the effective preaching of God's Word. Paul expressed the crucial role that preaching plays in salvation with these words to the church at Rome:

> For everyone who calls on the name of the Lord will be saved. But how can they call on Him in whom they have not believed? And how can they believe without hearing about Him? And how can they hear without a preacher? And how can they preach unless they are sent? As it is written: How welcome are the feet of those who announce the gospel of good things! (Romans 10:13-15, HCSB).

That such an incredible treasure as the forgiveness and eternal life offered through the Gospel should be communicated through the preaching of fallible humans is both amazing and sobering. Paul recognized the supreme irony of proclaiming the transcendent treasure of the Gospel though the "earthen vessels" or "clay jars" of human preachers (1 Corinthians 1:18-21, 2 Corinthians 4:7). Even so, God sovereignly chose preaching as the primary means of proclaiming the Gospel "so that this extraordinary power may be from God and not from us" (2 Corinthians 4:7, HCSB). It "pleased God by the foolishness of preaching to save them that believe" (1 Corinthians 1:21, KJV). Paul called upon Timothy (and every preacher) to "do the work of an evangelist" to "fulfill your ministry" (2 Timothy 4:5, HCSB). For this reason, a sound soteriology is crucial for the work of every preacher.

Preaching is not only important for the initiation into salvation (*justification*), but also our maturing in salvation (*sanctification*). In the Great Commission, Jesus commanded the church to "make disciples of all nations" by "teaching them to observe everything I have commanded you" (Matthew 28:19-20, HCSB). The early church in Jerusalem was discipled by the teaching of the apostles (Acts 2:42). In his last message to the elders of the church at Ephesus, the Apostle Paul reminded them that "for three years I did not cease night or day to admonish everyone with tears," ... "declaring to you the whole counsel of God" (Acts 20:27, 31, ESV). Ephesus was Paul's longest pastorate, and the apostle dedicated his preaching ministry to discipling the Ephesian church. The giftedness of pastors is described as being a "pastor/teacher" (Ephesians 4:11), being "apt to teach" is one of the qualifications for pastors (1 Timothy 3:2, 2 Timothy 2:24), and feeding the flock of God with sound doctrine is one of the key responsibilities of pastors (1 Timothy 3:2, 5:17; 2 Timothy 2:24, 4:1-4; Titus 1:9-16, 2:1; 1 Peter 5:2). Paul instructed Timothy, "Until I come, devote yourself to the public reading of Scripture, to preaching and to teaching [sound doctrine]" (1 Timothy 4:13, NIV). This task of teaching believers sound doctrine is a significant part of the responsibility of every pastor.

Ecclesiology: The Doctrine of the Church

Who should proclaim the Gospel and where should the primary locus be for Christian proclamation? The doctrine of the church (ecclesiology) is foundational for expository preaching for at least two reasons: because proclamation and discipleship are two of the major tasks of the church, and because of the preaching assignment given to the role of the pastor.

The five tasks of the New Testament church are often derived from the activities of the Jerusalem church as described in Acts 2 — witness, discipleship, fellowship, worship, and ministry. The church in Jerusalem was launched on the Day of Pentecost with Peter preaching the sermon at Pentecost (Acts 2:14-41). The church's *witness* brought a harvest of three thousand souls into the church on the day of Pentecost, and continued thereafter (Acts 2:37-41, 47). As persons were saved, they were led into *discipleship* by the teaching of the apostles (Acts 2:42). The church practiced *fellowship* by sharing meals and prayer daily — not merely social events, but "with gladness and sincerity of heart" in a profound spirit of *koinonia* (Acts 2:42, 46, NASB). The church's *worship* took place daily in the temple, as they praised God and experienced dramatic signs and wonders (Acts 2:43, 46-47). Finally, the church exemplified *ministry* by selflessly selling their own possessions to share with the needy (Acts 2:45). The act of preaching, of course, primarily helps fulfill the tasks of witness, worship, and discipleship. Since these are the basic tasks of the church, the crucial importance of proclamation in the church is very evident.

Who is to be the primary proclaimer in a local church? All Christians have the responsibility to witness, make disciples, and worship, of course, but the church's pastor is the person charged as the primary leader in this regard. The Bible describes the two offices of a New Testament church as pastor and deacon. The scriptural qualifications for ministry provide a basic job description for any ministry position, especially the pastor. As the undershepherd of the Great Shepherd, a pastor should reflect to some extent the three offices of Christ — prophet, priest, and king. These three offices overlap somewhat with the three main terms associated with the pastor's office in the New Testament— elder, pastor/shepherd, and bishop. The role of *elder* (*presbuteros,* 1 Peter 5:1) draws from the name of leaders in the Jewish tradition who provided wise counsel and teaching. The pastor/elder role is most associated with a trusted, experienced leader who provides wisdom and discernment in his teaching ministry. The role of a *pastor* or shepherd (*poimen,* 1 Peter 5:2) is most associated with providing pastoral care to shepherd the flock of God. The pastor/shepherd identifies with the people and cares lovingly for their needs. The role of a *bishop or overseer* (*episcopos,* 1 Peter 5:2) is most associated with exerting leadership and guidance for the congregation. The pastor/bishop should have oversight over the flock. Scripture clearly associates all three of these roles with the same office (1 Peter 5:1-2, Titus 1:5-7), which is most commonly called a *pastor* in most Southern Baptist churches.[24]

Each of these overlapping roles of the pastor include carrying out a *prophetic* ministry by proclaiming the Word of the Lord faithfully. A prophetic ministry is not primarily predictive, but is focused on teaching and proclaiming God's Word. The crucial importance of teaching in pastoral ministry is indicated by the fact that Scripture describes this Spirit-gifted role as pastor/teacher (Ephesians 4:11). The teaching role is specifically assigned to all three major synonyms for the role of pastor — bishop, elder, and pastor. Bishops/overseers should have an aptitude for teaching (1 Timothy 3:2; 2 Timothy 2:24; Titus 1:9). Likewise, elders are to minister in the Word and in doctrine (1 Timothy 5:17, Titus 1:9-16). Peter instructed his fellow elders to "feed the flock of God," language suggestive of both the elder and the pastor roles (1 Peter 5:2).

The priority of preaching is underscored throughout the New Testament. Citing Isaiah 61:1-2, Jesus described His own ministry of proclamation in His hometown synagogue, "The Spirit of the Lord is upon Me, because He has anointed Me to preach good news to the poor. He has sent Me to proclaim freedom to the captives and recovery of sight to the blind, to set free the oppressed, to proclaim the year of the Lord's favor" (Luke 4:18-19, HCSB).

Jesus went throughout the country preaching the Gospel of the kingdom of God (Matthew 4:17, 23; 11:1; Luke 4:43-44), and instructed His disciples to do the same (Matthew 10:7-20).

The first public work of the church was Peter's sermon at Pentecost (Acts 2:14-41). The office of deacons was established soon afterward so that the apostles could focus on a ministry of prayer and preaching (Acts 6:4). The preaching of the Gospel flourished (Acts 6:7) through the consistent preaching of the *kerygma* (the Gospel message of salvation through the cross of Christ) by early church leaders such as Peter, James, Stephen, and Philip (Acts 3:12-26; 4:8-20; 5:42; 6:8-7:60; 8:4-5, 35; 10:34-38; and 11:19-21).

Clearly, the Apostle Paul had a settled conviction about the centrality of preaching. He described preaching, rather than baptizing, as the primary focus of his ministry (1 Corinthians 1:17, 1 Timothy 2:7). In his missionary journeys, Paul and his team proclaimed the Gospel throughout the Gentile world (Acts 13:43-49; 17:1-4, 10-13, 22-34; 20:18-21). Paul was able to preach without hindrance even during his Roman imprisonment (Acts 28:31).

Preaching has always played a crucial role in the Christian church. The centrality of preaching was a hallmark of the Protestant Reformation, and has been characteristic in the Baptist tradition. However, some contemporary models of doing church seem to place a lower value on the role of preaching in the proclamation of the Gospel. A great need exists in our churches for a rediscovery of Bible-text based, God honoring, Christologically focused, Spirit empowered, and doctrinally sound expository preaching of the Word of God for the people of God. May God empower the preachers of this generation to rise to perform this sacred task with excellence, empowered by His Spirit!

Part III:
The Preacher as Pastor

Adam B. Dooley

The Importance of Biblical Preaching in Building a Great Church

by Adam B. Dooley

*I*n the latter part of the 20th century, no local pastor was more decidedly expositional in his preaching than Jerry Vines. The first time I heard him speak I was a mere 19 years old. Though the call of God on my life was still in infancy, the noticeable precision and passion of his Bible exposition forever altered the trajectory of my ministry. The historical-grammatical method of interpretation was foreign to me and I had no concept of Christ-centered ministry. Yet, listening to this faithful servant left me eager to walk systematically through the Bible in context while illustrating Scriptural significance for contemporary audiences. Between sessions at the First Baptist Church of Jacksonville Pastor's Conference, my mind raced as I tried to evaluate the message I heard. "I'm not sure what he just did or how he did it," I thought, "but that is exactly how I want to preach." Though I was unaware of topical preaching's deficiencies, this was my Warren Wiersbe -type moment that Dr. Vines experienced nearly fifty years ago.[1]

Little did I know that a few years later the preaching of Jerry Vines would anchor one more foundational conviction to my heart during the formative years of my ministry. After purchasing the *Heritage Series* tape collection at the St. Louis Southern Baptist Convention, I heard Dr. Vines' landmark sermon, *A Baptist and His Bible*, for the first time. Against the backdrop of the Conservative Resurgence, this message birthed a sense of stewardship within me that remains to this day. As a student of history, I knew that men like Paul Pressler, Paige Patterson, Adrian Rogers, Charles Stanley, and Jerry Vines believed that the future of our denomination depended upon a return to the Bible as the inspired, infallible, inerrant Word of God. I was only one year old when Pressler and Patterson launched what supporters have lovingly called the Battle for the Bible and opponents have venomously chided as the Fundamentalist Takeover from an Airport *Ramada Inn* in Atlanta, Georgia. Because of their efforts, however, I attended a seminary where:

The inerrancy of the Bible was celebrated rather than mocked.

The virgin birth was maintained and defended rather than diminished and discarded.

Genesis 1-11 was taught as literal history rather than theological fiction.

The bodily resurrection of Jesus Christ was heralded as the cornerstone of our faith.

The Gospel was not *a way* of salvation, but *THE way* of salvation.

Understandably, I was (and am) extremely grateful for the price that was paid by the architects and foot soldiers of this movement. While listening to Vines preach about the inerrancy of the Bible, however, I determined that I would not squander the sacrifice that was made for my generation. For me, this watershed message became the symbol of what was at stake as I handled the Scripture. I will never forget the poetic journey to the counseling room, classroom, and crisis room where we learned the intention, inspiration, and implications of the Bible. I sat in amazement as Dr. Vines identified the Old Thief of Destructive Criticism who uses a heretical hammer to drive the nails of anti-supernaturalism, a critical saw to divide the Scripture from the Word of God, and a cynical crowbar to pry God's Word from the hands of common people.

Perhaps it was naïveté, but at that moment I assumed that correct belief about the Bible would necessitate and facilitate consistent, careful use of the

Bible. That was then. Today, I am disconcertedly aware that the battle for the Bible continues, albeit in a slightly nuanced form. Though more subtle, the Bible's contemporary challenge is one of orthopraxy rather than orthodoxy. The Old Thief from a previous generation is still around, but he has new tools in his arsenal. Using a hostile hammer, he drives the nails of mockery to support the idea that Scripture can't possibly meet the needs of a sophisticated society. His secular saw strips the Bible of its relevance, maintaining it may be true but it is unnecessary to build a church. And with a compromising crowbar, he strips the Bible from the hands of the preacher in exchange for hip methods that lack Biblical substance. Consequently, despite maintaining a conviction about the inerrancy of Scripture, widespread confidence in the sufficiency of Scripture does not abound. The logical contradiction of professing inerrancy while practicing errancy plagues 21st century churches. Daniel Akin rightly warns, "Seduced by the sirens of modernity we have jettisoned a word-based ministry that is expository in nature, we have, in our attempt to be popular and relevant, become foolish and irrelevant. ... If the Bible is used at all, it is usually as proof-text out of context with no real connection to what the speaker is saying. Many who claim and perhaps believe they are expositors betray their confession by their practice."[2] Translation: We are walking the same dangerous path as our liberal counterparts from a generation ago, despite what we say we believe. In many circles, preaching is nothing more than a pop-psychology pep-rally and a felt-needs slobber-fest.

The words of Amos 8:11-12 are a sobering warning in this environment: "Behold, days are coming, declares the Lord God, When I will send a famine on the land, Not a famine for bread or a thirst for water, But rather for hearing the words of the Lord. People will stagger from sea to sea And from the north even to the east; They will go to and fro to seek the word of the Lord, But they will not find *it*."[3] The American pulpit desperately needs a return to basic, verse-by-verse exposition of the Scripture. If Bible inerrancy is a conviction of our hearts, then the Bible's sufficiency should be evident by the work of our hands.

Using his experience in the city of Thessalonica as a primary guide, I hope to demonstrate that the Apostle Paul had profound confidence in the sufficiency of the Scripture for building a great church. Certainly, a prominent theme of this epistle is the second coming of Jesus Christ. Two bookends, however, guide Paul's exhortations as he writes to the church that he loved so much. Everything the apostle says about these believers is based upon the fact that they "received the Word" (1:6). Then, before concluding the letter, Paul cautions them not to "despise prophetic utterances." These doorposts allow us to enter into the methodology of history's greatest missionary, only to discover his dependence on and confidence in the Scripture while doing ministry. What does 1 Thessalonians teach us about the sufficiency of the Bible?

The Bible Sufficiently Evangelizes Unbelievers

From beginning to end, the Bible proclaims the good news of salvation through Jesus Christ. Consequently, evangelizing the lost was at the heart of Paul's ministry, and his impact in Thessalonica demonstrates a methodology of evangelism that was saturated with Scripture. While establishing the church, God's missionary apostle "reasoned with them from the Scriptures" for three Sabbath days according to his custom (Acts 17:2). Furthermore, Acts 17:3 indicates that the focus of Paul's declaration was that Christ suffered, died, and rose again as God's promised Messiah. Paul identifies this message as "our gospel" in 1 Thessalonians 1:5, and then he explains that it came "not in word only, but also in power and in the Holy Spirit and with full conviction." God utilized the spoken word and the conviction of the messenger to powerfully transform many who heard. Thus, Acts 17:4 reports that "some of them were persuaded and joined Paul and Silas." 1 Thessalonians 2:1 celebrates, "For you yourselves know, brethren, that our coming to you was not in vain." Both Biblical content and Spirit power were important ingredients for proclaiming salvation.

Stated more practically, good things happen when a man preaches with a head full of Scripture and a heart that is passionate for God. While many mainstream denominations decry the continual decline of baptisms in our churches (and well we should), I fear that much of the preaching in many pulpits today does very little to point people to Jesus Christ. The Bible is not a book about having great relationships, building self-esteem, or obtaining financial success. It is, however, a sacred guide about how to find Jesus. 2 Timothy 3:15 assures us, "from childhood you have known the sacred writings which are able to give you the wisdom that leads to salvation through faith which is in Christ Jesus." Romans 10:17 says, "faith *comes* from hearing, and hearing by the word of Christ." Still, many reduce salvation to finding peace, happiness, or purpose in life. Though these goals have their place, this is not the message of the Bible. God's word is sufficient to meet the greatest need of every human heart when declared as it is written. Perhaps the greatest demonstration of this principle is found on the road to Emmaus during Jesus interaction with two men. Luke 24:27 says, "Beginning with Moses and with all the prophets, He explained to them the things concerning Himself in all the Scriptures." The impact of correct Biblical teaching is obvious in Luke 24:32 as these two men recall their experience, "Were not our hearts burning within us while He was speaking to us on the road, while He was explaining the Scriptures to us?" Later, Jesus appeared to the eleven disciples saying, "These are My words which I spoke to you while I was still with you, that all things which are written about Me in the Law of Moses and the Prophets and the Psalms must be fulfilled (Luke 24:44)." The Christological focus of the Bible makes it sufficient to evangelize unbelievers. Real Christian preaching will by necessity direct people to Jesus Christ because this is the fundamental goal of Scripture.

The Bible Sufficiently Disciples Believers

Believing that the Bible is sufficient for reaching the lost in no way diminishes the importance of Scripture in the life of a local congregation, particularly as it relates to those who are already Christ followers. Taking people deeper in their relationship with God is the natural effect of verse-by-verse teaching. Inspiring unbelievers and motivating mature believers cannot be reduced to stylistic gimmicks or shallow exhortation. Not only does the Bible sufficiently point people to salvation, but it also develops and matures every true Christ follower. Interestingly, after Paul indicates the Thessalonians received the word, he immediately cites evidence of their conversion. Chapter 1 of his letter is replete with practical manifestations that these believers were radically changed. He cites their "work of faith, labor of love, and steadfastness of hope" (1:2-3). With pastoral exuberance, Paul gratefully celebrates the Thessalonians imitation of his faith through their example to all believers (1:6), their Gospel witness (1:7), and their obedience to forsake idols in order to serve God. Interestingly, existence of these proofs was the result of their "having received the word" (1:6).

Apparently, passionately and consistently teaching the Scripture was Paul's method of discipleship. Much like a father caring for his children, he exhorted, encouraged, and implored this congregation with words of Divine inspiration (2:11). Consequently, these new believers grew rapidly in the faith. Note the emphasis on the word's activity within a Christian who receives it in 1 Thessalonians 2:13, "For this reason we also constantly thank God that when you received the word of God which you heard from us, you accepted *it* not *as* the word of men, but *for* what it really is, the word of God, which also performs its work in you who believe." No wonder the standard of faithfulness is the continual adherence to the revealed word of God. When writing to the Thessalonians the second time, Paul reminded them to stand fast and hold firmly to the sound doctrine of holy writ regardless of how they received it (tradition, words, or his letters) (2 Thessalonians 2:15).

Furthermore, 1 Thessalonians 4:1-3 offers a pointed example of how the Bible can be a means of sanctification. After reminding them that his instructions and commandments (Scripture) were given by the authority of Jesus, Paul pleads with the Thessalonians to abstain from sexual immorality. Aside from the issue addressed, we immediately notice the appeal to inspired directives for moral and ethical norms. Living under the authority of the Bible will keep an individual on the path of sanctified righteousness. Elsewhere, Paul states it this way, "All Scripture is inspired by God and profitable for teaching, for reproof, for correction, for training in righteousness; so that the man of God may be adequate, equipped for every good work" (2 Timothy 3:16-17).

In addition to serving as an impetus of sanctification, the Bible also promises believers future glorification. How does this relate to the issue of sufficiency? Eternal priorities replace temporal ambitions when a person genuinely obeys the word. Illustrating this reality emerges as a practical theme throughout 1 Thessalonians. Because these believers received the word, they turned from idols "to wait for His Son from heaven, whom He raised from the dead, *that is* Jesus, who rescues us from the wrath to come" (1:10). Paul assures the Thessalonians of their participation in the Lord's return by teaching the resurrection of the dead and the rapture of the living in 1 Thessalonians 4:13-18. Interestingly, he invokes "the word of the Lord" (4:15) and concludes his thought by saying "comfort one another with these words" (4:18). Elsewhere, Scripture focuses us on the eschatological reality that we shall be like Him, for we shall see Him as He is (1 John 3:2). It assures us that the Lord Jesus will transform our lowly bodies to be remade according to His glorious body (Philippians 3:21). Likewise, the Bible inspires us that every knee will bow and every tongue will confess that Jesus Christ is Lord to the glory of God the Father (Philippians 2:10-11).

With a closed canon at our disposal, Paul's methodology is both informative and instructive. God's primary means for changing people's lives is found within the pages of His word. Assuming that a preacher is wise enough to put his finger on the greatest spiritual priorities in a person's life is the great fallacy of felt-needs preaching. A steady diet of Biblical exposition is critically important not only because it holds preachers accountable to teach all the Scripture, but also because it allows the Holy Spirit to address issues that ignorance, cowardice, or self-preservation would not beckon us to broach. Refusing to declare the whole counsel of God communicates that the Bible is not the objective standard for life and should be ignored (lacks inerrancy), OR that the Bible is the objective standard for life but we should not care (lacks sufficiency). Neither are acceptable.

The Bible Sufficiently Prepares Preachers

Observing the sustained impact of Paul's ministry among the Thessalonians captures the exhortative power intrinsic to the word. To contrast, Paul reminds them that his exhortation did "not come from error," his motive lacked "impurity," and his methodology was void of "deceit" (2:3). There was an accuracy, purity, and persuasiveness to what he said that reflected a message from God. Far from faulty reasoning, the message of Paul was resounded with the supernatural power of inspiration and inerrancy. The persecutor turned preacher was not seeking to make a name for himself by means of human applause or approval. Additionally, his methodology was safe from manipulative tactics. All of this drives us to a central question that every preacher should ask. Why was Paul so careful when he preached? And why should preachers today do likewise?

The answer to these questions lies in the privilege of the preaching assignment. Paul understood that teaching the Bible is a sacred duty whereby God entrusts a messenger and empowers a message. Those called to preach are "approved by God" and "entrusted with the gospel" (2:4). Though some diminish the importance of calling, the language of stewardship reminds us that God uniquely prepares certain individuals for this task. Despite the frailties of the messenger, a pure vessel is permitted to take the word of God, empowered by the Spirit of God, to stand before the people of God, as an ambassador of God, and direct others to the will of God. Outside of personal salvation, there is no greater privilege! No wonder 2 Timothy 2:15 cautions, "Be diligent to present yourself approved to God as a workman who does not need to be ashamed, accurately handling the word of truth." Thus, "pleasing men" and seeking "glory from men" was unnecessary when Paul preached (2:4, 6). Yet, the Thessalonians accepted his teaching not as the word of men, but as the word of God (2:13). Because his agenda was declaring what they needed to hear rather than discerning what they wanted to hear, Paul's preaching among the Thessalonians was a means of changing lives. Our assignment is no different.

Balancing the ever-changing demands of people with Biblical fidelity remains an unachievable goal. Despite widespread pressure from the pew to shape the pulpit, God is still calling Spirit-filled messengers to supply what most listeners do not even know they need. This approach will not come without consequence, however, due to growing pressure to acquiesce to the demands of the culture. Fortunately, two statements within 1 Thessalonians make it clear that Paul's approach does not require compromise in order to achieve relevance. He pleads, "We request of you, brethren, that you appreciate those who diligently labor among you, and have charge over you in the Lord and give you instruction (5:12)." And he cautions, "Do not despise prophetic utterances" (5:20). The last thing a lukewarm 21st century church needs is a pastor who caves under pressures, caters his message to special interest groups, and compromises his principles for popularity. Ultimately, the standard of successful preaching is not the critique from the pew, the comparison of another pulpit, or the confidence of your own perspective. Because we serve an audience of one, honoring God with faithful exegesis and proclamation must be our primary concern. To help us focus, 1 Thessalonians 2:4 concludes with the solemn reminder that it is "God who examines our hearts." Sermons possessing the wrong message, motive, or method are easily detected by the One to whom we must give an account. While I don't diminish that standing before people who readily respond to you a number of ways can be a fearful thing, even more frightening is the evaluation of heaven after failing to preach the word you said God called you to divide. As much as I lie awake at night and wonder how people must evaluate my preaching, the most sobering exercise is always considering what

God thinks of it. Aiming to please people while preaching disrespects a holy God and forfeits the sacred calling of the pulpit. Because Paul's preaching strategy allowed the Scripture to determine the parameters of his message, the purity of his motive, and the power of his methodology, we can trust that it will sufficiently prepare us as well. Despite the onslaught of public scrutiny and criticisms, the Bible focuses our ambition toward the approval of the One who called us.

The Bible Sufficiently Comforts the Hurting

Born out of tremendous tribulation and suffering, the lessons of 1 Thessalonians also remind us that Scripture adequately provides comfort in the midst of great difficulties. Having already observed how the Thessalonians received the word, it is worth noting that they did so amid "much tribulation" (1:6). In fact, their hardship was perhaps the greatest indicator they accepted the word (2:13-15). To be sure they were not discouraged by their afflictions, Paul sent Timothy to minister the word to the Thessalonians (3:2-4). The mood of the contemporary church implies that if you really love God and live for Him you will never have any problems, leaving many Christians feeling abandoned by God. Yet, Paul repeatedly warned these believers that trials were inevitable and reminded them they were "destined for this" (3:3). The message of the Bible is not that Christians can walk with God *without* any trouble, but that they do so *despite* any trouble. Thus, in 1 Thessalonians 3:10 Paul expressed a desire to "complete what was lacking in their faith." The overall tone of the epistle does not suggest a faith deficiency here, but a sincere desire to enhance faith that was already present. Realizing that their suffering required continual dependence upon God, Paul longed to encourage the Thessalonians by means of the Scripture. Despite their hardship, he admonished them to continue walking and excelling according to the "instruction" they received (4:1). Sustained suffering requires sustained reliance upon God through His word.

God is teaching me these truths in a personal way during this season of my life. On July 10, 2011, my family received devastating news that challenged everything I believe and teach. After a week of traveling, my wife and I were concerned about unusual red dots, forming a strange rash on my oldest son Carson's neck. On Sunday, my wife took him to see our pediatrician while I went to church for the morning service. Ironically, I finished a series through the Sermon on the Mount that day by telling our congregation that storms are a reality and they reveal who we really are. Shortly after the service, I joined the family for a bite of lunch while we waited for test results from the doctor. This is when things started to change rapidly. When the nurse called she refused to give us the test results over the phone. We knew it was bad when she met us at the door and suggested that she watch our children while we talked to the doctor. I will never forget how my heart broke and my spirit wept when she said the word leukemia. My precious, firstborn son had leukemia.

Through a whirlwind of activity, we were checking into St. Jude Children's Research Hospital in Memphis, Tennessee, by 10:30 p.m. After a sleepless night of listening to doctors and signing waivers, I felt as though I was about to buckle under the pressure of it all. Then, on a webpage created for friends to encourage us, I read a simple message from a young man in our church. After assuring us of his prayers, he simply attached a verse from the sermon I preached just hours before. Matthew 7:25 reads, "And the rain fell, and the floods came, and the winds blew and slammed against that house; and yet it did not fall, for it had been founded on the rock." Supernaturally, God used His word to assure me that I would not crack or fall during this trial because He was my rock. In the days that followed, God repeatedly drove me to various Scriptures. I read Job 1:21, "Naked I came from my mother's womb, And naked I shall return there. The Lord gave and the Lord has taken away. Blessed be the name of the Lord" and Job 2:10, "Shall we indeed accept good from God and not accept adversity?" Through these verses and many others, God continues to show me that His word is sufficient when we face difficulties.

If that were not enough, the end of Paul's ministry also teaches us that the Bible is sufficient for life's greatest trial. Just weeks before his death, I can see the apostle Paul, lying in a Roman prison cell, his back covered with the stripes of his scourging all because he refused to stop preaching the Gospel. There is a small ray of light that shines dimly through a crack in the wall. It is barely enough illumination for the apostle to see his hand in front of his face, but it will do. Paul feels for something to write with by running his hand over the floor as the rattle of his chains follows his arm across the room. Finally he has it, so he lies on his stomach with his face just an inch from the floor in order to see what he writes. And what will he write? The apostle gathers his thoughts and narrows them down to the single most important issue, the one ingredient of ministry that Timothy must never forget. And so, with great compulsion, he writes, "*PREACH THE WORD.*"

Strange instruction when you consider the fact that he had already been beaten, shipwrecked, and imprisoned for his preaching. Now, just before paying the ultimate price for his bold, uncompromising declarations, Paul admonishes his protégé to do the very thing that leads to his earthly demise. How are we to make sense of this seemingly reckless expectation? Paul understood that Scripture is the only sufficient means for building a great church, and thus, considered any price to share it with others a necessary sacrifice. So, just after his bold imperative, the aged ambassador insists that Timothy "reprove, rebuke, exhort, with great patience and instruction" (2 Timothy 4:2), having already reminded him that "all Scripture is inspired of God and profitable for teaching, for reproof, for correction, for training in righteousness" (2 Timothy 3:16). In other words, the Bible is sufficient for discipleship. After stressing the need to preach the word against the backdrop of false doctrine (2 Timothy 4:3-4), Paul implores the young pastor to "do the work of the evangelist" just one verse later (2 Timothy 4:5). Stated differently, the Bible is sufficient for evangelism. Lest the daunting nature of this task bewilder Timothy, Paul encourages him that because all Scripture is inspired of God, "the man of God may be adequate, equipped for every good work" (2 Timothy 3:17). No wonder he believed the Bible is sufficient to prepare preachers for ministry. Finally, just after announcing that his death was imminent (2 Timothy 4:6-8), Paul pleads with Timothy to come soon to him soon, bringing his books, but "especially the parchments" (2 Timothy 4:13). He understood, as should we, that the Bible is sufficient to comfort those who are hurting, even as they face death. Brothers, the Bible has always been and will always be ... sufficient.

Biblical Preaching in a Mega-Church Setting

by Mac Brunson

*I*n August 1862, General John Pope's army marched at a feverish pace day after day. They later discovered they had been marching in circles the entire time. All they had accomplished in the end was out-marching their supplies, leaving themselves hungry and exhausted. To make matters even worse, the soldiers had lost confidence in their general who, truthfully, had no idea where the Confederate forces were located. All of this foreshadowed defeat. When Pope's troops finally faced the highly decorated Thomas "Stonewall" Jackson Division, they fully expected to be whipped.[1] Thankfully, in the arena of preaching, people who sit under the teaching of Dr. Jerry Vines need not worry about being misled, as General's Pope's troops were, going round and around in confusion. Those whom he pastored, and those of us who sat under his preaching, know with certainty that Dr. Vines will carefully exegete the text with the precision of a sharpshooter and the skill of a surgeon.

Preaching in a mega-church setting is really no different than preaching in any other venue. The reason is simple: people need to hear a word from God. Regardless of the size of the congregation or the number of seats in the auditorium, people ponder one question: is there a word from God that addresses my life? People *in* every age need the Word of God; people *of* every age need the Word of God. Regrettably, too much has been made of mega-churches as if they were a new phenomenon and deserve unique treatment. We tend to forget that when the church was born at Pentecost it would have been considered a mega-church since three-thousand were converted. Clearly, the church was birthed out of the "preaching event." In light of this, one has to wonder if Peter walked into a church today would he recognize the "preaching event." Certainly, there would have been no question if the great apostolic preacher of Pentecost had walked into a service at First Baptist Jacksonville during the tenure of Jerry Vines.

Priority Of Preaching

In his excellent book entitled, *Preaching and Preachers,* Martin Lloyd-Jones wrote:

> ... I would say without hesitation that the most urgent need in the Christian Church is true preaching; and as it is the greatest need in the Church, it is obviously the greatest need in the world also.[2]

Vines would agree with Lloyd-Jones. The greatest demand in the church and in the world today is true preaching of God's Word. That is why preaching was the priority for Vines as a pastor. When we look back at the proclamation of the Old Testament prophets we discover that it was rooted in God's Word. Likewise in the New Testament we observe that preaching was rooted in the "Gospel," in Jesus Christ and His finished work. Paul summarized this theme in a letter to the Corinthians:

> And I, brethren, when I came to you, came not with excellency of speech or of wisdom, declaring unto you the testimony of God. For I determined not to know anything among you, save Jesus Christ, and Him crucified. (1 Corinthians 2:1-2 KJV).

Preaching in any setting, mega church or in a tent with a sawdust covered floor, must be rooted in God's Word and the Gospel of Jesus Christ. The central message, the primacy of preaching for apostolic preaching was the person and work of Jesus Christ. The day of Pentecost illustrates this truth. Of all the things that could have been done at the church's inception, preaching was the primary event. When you stop and think of all that the Holy Spirit could have done through Peter with thousands of Jews gathered that day, it is striking to note what the Holy Spirit saw as a priority. He could have dictated church polity. He could have directed a lesson on church constitutions and by-laws. In addition, the Spirit could have led them all in a singing of the psalms, or in a concert of new music, or in a lecture on the dangers of Jewish liberalism. But the Spirit did not choose to emphasize any of these important aspects of church life. Instead, He infused Peter with power to preach. Peter took a text from Joel and expounded on its fulfillment in Jesus Christ. From there Peter focused on the life, cross, and the resurrection of Jesus Christ. Peter's sermon ended with a very pointed application. The listeners had crucified the Son of God who God Himself had raised from the dead. It was then and there that Peter issued a bold call for repentance:

> Then Peter said unto them, Repent, and be baptized every one of you in the name of Jesus Christ for the remission of sins, and ye shall receive the gift of the Holy Ghost. (Acts 2:38 KJV).

This is the *kerygma*, the preaching event. It was the priority of the Holy Spirit, the emphasis of Peter, the primacy of Paul, and the heart of apostolic preaching. Furthermore, preaching was the nucleus of Jerry Vines' ministry as pastor and must be the priority of every pastor regardless of church size.

Principles Of Preparation

When preaching serves as the priority of the pastor, then preparation becomes the primary focus of his time. A pastor's schedule is demanding, and ever more so in this day, but he must not neglect the diligent study of God's Word. In fact, sermon preparation must be given precedence above everything else. Many pastors would disagree and argue that pastoral ministry comes first. Those who say that overlook the fact that preaching is pastoral ministry in its highest fashion. Years ago, Wally Amos Criswell once stated that more pastoral ministry could be done from the pulpit than could ever be done one-on-one with a congregation. Considering this, there is no greater task for the pastor than to handle accurately the Word of God. Moving the Word of God out of the "then" and into the "now" is vital in communicating the Gospel of Jesus Christ to the people. The sermon process begins with the text. Vines is a master of exegesis and his style is so classically expositional that his sermons, like cream, rise to the top. He gives great attention to context, which is the first step to the historico-grammatical interpretation for preaching.

A canonical context locates the passage in the larger flow of Biblical revelation, followed by the book's setting (book context) and then the immediate background (again context). Vines does not give yawn provoking lectures on ancient history but sets the context precisely like apples of gold in settings of silver.

Vines' sermons also reflect careful research given to the grammatical elements of a text. Exposition of scripture is not exposition unless it gives careful attention to morphology, the form of words, and lexicology, the meaning of the words. Vines' command of language study became apparent to the writer one night when he took his iPad and highlighted a Greek text and began to read, translate, and discuss the verbs and nouns of the passage and how they related to one another syntactically. One would be hard pressed to find a single sermon where Vines did not discuss the *usus loquendi*, the meaning of the words at the time of the writing of the text, and their significance in grasping what the author was saying.

Vines does not offer linguistic pearls to his listeners merely for intellectual entertainment. In fact, all of this technical exposition would be incomplete without application of the text. Anyone who has ever heard Vines preach knows that he never shies away from strong, Biblical, pointed application of the text. Application of the text is essential for sermons because it is the precise point where the rubber hits the road. A sermon void of application fails at the point of the prophetic and if ever there was a prophetic voice in our generation, it is Dr. Vines.

Passion is critical to application. It is where the preacher demonstrates how the exposition has moved him personally. Passion demonstrates that the preacher has met the Master in the text. In fact, application reveals two things about the preacher. First, it exposes his passion for the Word of God; and second, it demonstrates his passion for the lost. While exposition shows a pastor's love for the Lord and his congregation, in the application you see the pastor's passion for the Word and for the lost.

Those four things are critical elements that make up the preaching of Jerry Vines in every church situation. As a pastor, and now as an itinerate evangelist, his love for the Lord and for the church is obvious in how carefully he handles the exposition of a text. His passion for the Word of God and for the lost is legendary.

The critical issue in preaching the authoritative Word of God is that the preacher must have already surrendered his life to the authority of the Word he preaches. When it comes to the preaching of Vines, this is not an issue. In fact, he is perhaps one of the most "surrendered" men to have ever stepped into a pulpit. What has been true of him in small country churches applies to him in intermediate size churches, and is true of him in mega church settings. The size of the church did not influence his willingness to preach, his intensity in preaching, or his dedication to the Word of God. There has been no oscillation, vacillation, or equivocation of being faithful to preach the Word of God depending on the size of the various churches he has pastored or numerous places he has preached.

It would be difficult to determine the number of hours that Vines spends crafting one single sermon but it is sufficient to say it is prodigious. Dr. Vines understands that while God certainly attends our preparation, He expects us to diligently labor over the truth in prayer and study. Then, we can stand with bold assurance that God will bring the fire.

Personal Price

At some point, every pastor has prayed the prayer of Moses in Exodus 33:18:

I pray thee, show me Thy glory.

There is a yearning in a pastor's heart, a yawning chasm that longs to be filled with the glory of God. Moses had just gone through an horrific experience when the people he was leading had turned completely on the commitment they had made to the Lord and fell down to worship a golden calf. It is certain that Moses was angry, hurt, frustrated, and fostered a sense of failure and the feelings of "how can I go on?" He wanted to get back to the mountain with God and away from the people. Moses surely dealt with the sense of inadequacy, discouragement, and even despair and what he wanted more than anything else was to see God's glory.

It costs something to enter God's presence. Paul tells us in 1 Corinthians 6:19-20 that we are not our own, we have been bought with a price. Because of sin, it cost God His beloved Son to make it possible for us to stand in His presence and experience His grace. On the other hand, a price must also be paid by preachers. In Luke 14 Jesus talks about counting the cost for those who would follow Him:

> If anyone comes to Me and does not hate ... even his own life, he cannot be My disciple. Anyone who does not carry his cross and follow me cannot be my disciple. (Luke 14:26-27)

No one knows this personal price any better than Dr. Vines.

The first price the pastor so often pays is sacrificing time with his spouse and his children. Every pastor and his family know the price to be paid for ministry. Notwithstanding church size, the pastor's family often suffers the most. Beside the time for preparation, administration, and visitation of all the other families in and out of the church, the pastor's family sees little of their husband and father.

Next there is the congregational price that has to be paid. Imagine a compass with north, south, east, and west on it. The pastor normally finds himself in the middle position of the compass. He is always under pressure to run in all four directions at the same time. Congregations, regardless of size, can be so demanding that the pressure becomes overwhelming.

The third price to be paid is the spiritual price. Satan slings one missile after another hoping something is going to hit. Pastors are faced not just with the usual sins that everyone battles with, but there is especially in the ministry a pull toward self-indulgence, laziness, discouragement, and pride.

In addition to the price spiritually, there is a personal price to be paid. Any pastor who preaches the Word will pay a price at some point for taking a Biblical stand. Someone somewhere will be offended by the truth in general and some people in the church will be upset in particular. This is a common experience for pastors regardless of church size. A mega-church does not reduce the certainty and level of upset but perhaps exacerbates the difficulty. The bigger the church, the bigger the target painted on the pastor's back and the larger the pool of discontented congregants. God's call to ministry does not come with an exemption from trouble, attacks, hurts, and misunderstandings. Christ's summons to follow Him always includes the invitation to come and die. Dietrich Bonhoeffer said, "When Christ calls a man, he bids him come and die."[3] Peter tells us that Christ bore our sins in His body on the cross so that we might die to sin, (1 Peter 2:24). However, when we die to that sin, whether it is greed, laziness, self-indulgence, anger, or coldness, we experience God's glory in our lives.

As a pastor and preacher, Jerry Vines experienced the cost of ministry. He has paid the price personally, spiritually, individually, and in family life. Vines has done it with great grace and dedication to the Lord, his wife, family, denomination, and congregation. It is impossible to enter into the circle of esteemed preachers in the latter half of the twentieth century and first half of the twenty-first century like he has, without paying a high price to sustain marriage, family, and self together with dignity and godliness.

Over the past six years, Dr. Vines and I have communicated on a weekly basis. So often he will be preaching in a small country church, but he will be excited to share his sermon outline, his points, his application, and his expositional work as if he were headed off to preach at Charles Spurgeon's Metropolitan Tabernacle. This says much about him personally. It gives great insight into his motivation and validates why he is considered a prince of exposition in our day. The size of the church does not dictate the amount of preparation Vines goes through, the intensity of passion Vines preaches with or the level of price he is willing to pay to preach the Word of God. Vines retains the same high standard for God's Word, and for God's church, and for the preaching event no matter where he ministers. No pastor should ever consider doing any less because of the numbers in the audience.

John A. Broadus knew the importance of preparation and was willing to pay the price. It is said that Broadus prepared, wrote, and delivered his lectures that we know as his classic work *On the Preparation and Delivery of Sermons* to one lone, blind student. Perhaps we would not view one student as a wise investment of time, but history shows us what God has done with those lectures in the lives of countless ministers in the years since. Every preacher in essence preaches to an audience of One —and it should be the best he can preach.

Approximately five centuries have passed since the great Erasmus wrote his preface to the Greek New Testament. That text became the basis for the King James Version of the Bible, which literally became the grammar for the English speaking world. It has been the standard for ministerial study ever since. His preface stated:

These holy pages will summon up the living image of Christ's mind. They will give you Christ Himself, talking, healing, dying, rising — the whole Christ, in a word. They will give Him to you in an intimacy so close that He would be less visible to you if He stood before your eyes.[4]

That has been the preaching of Dr. Vines in any and every church setting. He has honored the Word, lifted up the Gospel, preached Jesus Christ, at times so passionately, that *Jesus could be less visible if He stood right before your eyes.*

Part IV:
The Preacher as Evangelist

Jeff Pennington

Do The Work Of An Evangelist

by Jeff Pennington

I first met and interviewed Jerry Vines in the fall of 2006 at his favorite Starbucks coffee shop in Canton, Georgia. The intersection of my life with his could not have occurred at a more beneficial time. Dr. Vines had recently retired from his historic tenure as pastor of First Baptist Church, Jacksonville, Florida. After retiring he had some time to give, and I was in search of a dissertation topic that brought together preaching and evangelism. The research and relationship that began in that first interview not only led to graduation, but it also became one of the most advantageous classrooms of my eleven year seminary career. What I gained along the way was more than academic in nature, it marked me for life.

This chapter's topic gives me the opportunity to speak to one of the most striking aspects of Vines' ministry. For years he has rightfully garnered the reputation as one who preaches the Word. Anyone familiar with his pulpit ministry understands why Carl L. Kell and L. Raymond Camp use an old southern folklore to give his preaching a ringing endorsement: "If you don't want to believe the man, don't listen to him."[1] Furthermore, those who know of his role in the Conservative Resurgence are not likely surprised that Vines' clearest recollection of his ordination service is that of his grandfather, the country-evangelist W.O. Johnson, breaking down in tears and praying that his grandson would be true to the Bible.[2] Along with being an exemplary expositor and champion for inerrancy, his entire pastoral career was marked by steadfast evangelistic focus. Out of humility he never calculated the sum total of the baptisms tallied during his pastorates, but for research purposes I discovered that figure to exceed 23,000 people.[3]

The pages that follow describe the commitments that Vines persistently fulfilled that led thousands to experience new birth in Christ. His evangelistic efforts were directed by the irresistible logic of the Bible. Rarely was he outpaced in his commitment to personal evangelism. He preached and taught through the Book of Acts to disciple his church members to engage in "Continual Lifestyle Evangelism." He masterfully used his "evangelistic twist" within nearly every pastoral preaching opportunity. Jerry Vines' ministry is paradigmatic in the present milieu of evangelistic ineffectiveness because he preached the Word, and he did the work of an evangelist.

The Irresistible Logic of the Bible

Two correlative qualities emerge when one traces Vines' pastoral ministry from start to finish. He matured as both an expositor and an evangelist. It is not coincidental that the evangelistic fruitfulness of his ministry, measured in annual baptisms, increased when he made a full commitment to expository preaching.[4] The relationship is so strong, in fact, that I am persuaded that his commitment to expository preaching is largely responsible for his strikingly persistent commitment to sharing the Gospel.

Vines' method of sermon preparation was the agent that brought these two qualities together. Five mornings each week he would begin studying around 6:00 a.m. His first forty-five minutes involved devotional Bible reading and prayer. Then, until 11:00 a.m., he engaged in the careful study of the Bible.[5] The effect that this study had on Vines was immeasurable. His mastery of the Bible empowered his preaching, but it also produced an uncanny evangelistic focus. In his study he daily grappled with what he still calls "the irresistible logic of the Bible." This logic stems from the Great Commission (Matthew 28:19-20), but its basis involves much more. He finds this logic throughout the entirety of Scripture underlying any text the Spirit directs him to study as he prepares to preach. Sometimes he calls it "the irresistible logic of the church," and other times he references it as "the irresistible logic of evangelism." No matter his nomenclature, its content remains the same:

If there is a heaven and there is, and if there is a hell and there is, and if Jesus died on the cross to make it possible for people to go to heaven[6] and to not go to hell, then the most important business of the church is to let people know that they do not have to go to hell, they can go to heaven. Because Jesus died on the cross for their sins it is possible for them to go to heaven.

This logic is what gave Vines' evangelistic focus its priority. Even when he was called to devote large amounts of time to sermon preparation, counseling, administration, staff, deacon/committee meetings, hospital visitation, home visitation, denominational life, and a litany of other matters, his commitment to evangelism was given top-tier primacy. Calvin Carr, who served with him as a youth minister at First Baptist Church, Jacksonville, Florida, remembers the commitment to personal evangelism that his irresistible logic produced: "Dr. Vines modeled a heart for evangelism. He went visiting every week, even during the time he was president of the SBC and he was very busy."[7] Nelson Sturgill, a former chairman of the deacons at First Baptist Jacksonville, speaks to the way the logic was perceived in his preaching: "Dr. Vines has had a great impact on our family. We feel very fortunate to have been under his leadership and ministry for the last twenty-three years. We could always be sure if we brought a visitor, they would hear the plan of salvation and have an opportunity to accept Christ."[8] Every witnessing opportunity, along with every sermon Vines preached, gave him the opportunity to engage in a Christian's greatest assignment.

A Commitment to Personal Evangelism

Fueled by his conviction of the irresistible logic of the Bible, Vines persisted throughout his ministry as an exemplary personal evangelist. This commitment affected his own life, but it also contributed to what he calls the "soul consciousness" of the churches he pastored.[9] Consider the implications for personal evangelism for both pastor and congregation found in Vines' appeal for a preacher's integrity: "The Bible makes very clear that the preacher preaches by his life as well as by his lips: there is a sense in which what a man *is* is more important than what he says. There is great strength in the silent sermon of a godly life."[10] A necessary solvent in the solution for a faithful minister of the Gospel is his authentic living. Especially does this solution hold true for a minister with precise evangelistic focus. Vines lived as a model of personal evangelism for his people, and it gave him credibility when he urged his members to do likewise.

Even as a teenager Vines evidenced a commitment to personal evangelism. He admitted to being gripped with fear when he considered the prospect of trying to lead someone to Christ, but he overcame that fear and led two boys to Christ in a housing project in Carrollton, Georgia. Vines remembers, "When I led them to Christ, and then when I saw them baptized at the main church that Sunday night, it just absolutely put the fire in my bones. I mean, I found a joy there, that I have never known and that I wanted to experience from now on, that I've never really gotten away from."[11]

The joy he wanted to repeatedly experience became a regular, reoccurring reality. As the pastor of Second Baptist Church in Cedartown, Georgia (1965), his evangelistic zeal pushed him to average 30 visits each Saturday while preaching morning and evening services on Sunday. The fruit of his devotion yielded 110 baptisms in that year alone.[12] The following years he served as pastor of West Rome Baptist Church in Rome, Georgia (1968-1974). There he birthed a deaf ministry, a bus ministry, a children's church service, and a church bookstore. He served as the chaplain for the West Rome High School football team, and even hosted a radio program called, *What's the Good Word?*[13] "Those were good years," Vines said as he reminisced, and understandably so. He led the church to average 111 baptisms per year.[14] While he served Dauphin Way Baptist in Mobile, Alabama as pastor (1974-1979), the church averaged 251 baptisms.[15]

Most recently, as the co-pastor/pastor of First Baptist Church, Jacksonville, Florida (1982-2006), Vines experienced his most extensive evangelistic fruitfulness. The church averaged 835 baptisms per year.[16] As he did the work of the evangelist he also equipped the churches he served to do the same (2 Timothy 4:5, Ephesians 4:10). Following Vines and Homer Lindsay Jr.'s leadership, over 2,000 First Baptist members constituted the church's evangelistically-driven Sunday School leadership. The weekly visitation program regularly averaged over 1,000 participants.[17] By November of 1989, the church was ministering to over 15,000 individuals enrolled in Sunday School.[18]

Throughout these years of pastoral ministry Vines would lead his church's visitation ministry, but his commitment to personal evangelism was not confined to this ministry alone. Daily he prayed for God to give him opportunities to share his faith. These prayers were often answered with a person's conversion. For instance, in a correspondence with Leavell Landrum, a former president of New Orleans Baptist Theological Seminary, he shared:

> I appreciate your commitment to pray for me. I am glad you are joining me in a commitment to soul-winning. Yesterday, I had the joy of leading a cab driver in Washington, D.C., to the Lord Jesus. It's thrilling when the Lord gives us an "along the way." Tonight, I am going out to visit a young couple that needs the Lord. I pray I will be able to win them to Christ.[19]

This commitment to personal evangelism was palpable to the congregations he led, and many under his leadership, staff and laity included, submitted to the same irresistible logic of the Bible that directed their pastor's life.

Perhaps the finest example of his evangelistic fidelity occurred at the time of his retirement. Janet Vines shared with me of an encounter that she and Vines had with a neighboring couple the day they left Jacksonville, Florida to relocate to Canton, Georgia. Though the husband was a Christian, the wife had never professed Christ. She paid the Vines a parting visit, and while doing so, she prayed to receive Christ. After observing her neighbors for years, the consistency of their life and witness became the instrument God used to lead her to saving faith. After recalling the story with great affection, Mrs. Vines quipped, "That was something I got to enjoy. He probably has a thousand just like it."[20]

"Continual Lifestyle Evangelism" from the Book of Acts

Vines' persistent commitment to personal evangelism was a tool that God used to equip the saints to do the work of the ministry, but that was just part of the way he trained his church members evangelistically. He also transferred his evangelistic focus through his preaching and teaching of the Book of Acts. He stated in an interview, "When I went to a church, I would start a series in the book of Acts and a lot of people bought into it."[21] Additionally, for nearly two decades he developed and authored Sunday

School curriculum entitled *Acts Alive* that taught evangelistic principles from Acts through small group Bible study.[22] The impetus for his evangelistic training curriculum is clear and persuasive. Since the irresistible logic of the Bible prioritizes evangelism as a Christian's most important assignment, the most strategic time to train church members in this assignment is during the time that yielded the most participants. At First Baptist Church Jacksonville, Florida, that time was Sunday School.

Vines introduces his *Acts Alive* curriculum with the principle that "Acts is intended to make us personal witnesses."[23] As much as any other book in the Bible, Acts trains and motivates people to do the work that he calls "continuous lifestyle evangelism."[24] His definition of lifestyle evangelism differs from Joe Aldrich who reasons, "The words of the Gospel are to be incarnated before they can be verbalized."[25] Aldrich's approach leads to the belief that one must first have a relationship with a non-believer before the Gospel can be shared. Vines affirms the evangelistic benefits that relationships with non-believers carry, but what he calls "continuous lifestyle evangelism" is quite different. He defines it as an intentional effort to make Gospel proclamation an integral part of a believer's everyday living.

Applications of Acts for Personal Evangelism

Vines' insights from Acts that unleashed his church to practice "continuous lifestyle evangelism" are especially helpful, for they transcend the restraints of a particular time and culture. They contextualize well in almost any ministry setting because they enable all Christians everywhere to obediently fulfill their responsibilities as personal evangelists. What follows is a sampling of some of the main principles that First Baptist Jacksonville "bought into" that attributed to the church's consistent evangelistic fruitfulness.

A Christian's Most Important Activity is to Witness. Foundational to continual lifestyle evangelism is the responsibility God gives every believer to be a witness. The Great Commission passage of Acts 1:8 is normative for all Christians. Thus, Jesus' imperative to be a witness is not a suggestion, it is a command. Through witnessing a believer lives out normal Christianity. A witness is "someone who has experienced something and can tell about it."[26] Like a witness in a courtroom that is sworn in to tell the truth, a witness for Jesus has received Christ as Savior, is changed by Jesus, and now lives a better life. As he witnesses, he tells others what Jesus means to him.[27]

Acts 1:13-26 discusses the essential preparations for witnessing. The disciples' example of spending ten days in prayer before Pentecost demonstrates how necessary it is for a believer committed to lifestyle evangelism to engage in daily prayer. Furthermore, a witness must be a person who believes, much like Peter, that the Bible "speaks with fresh power today." In order for Judas to be replaced, Peter's knowledge of Scripture demonstrated how the Scriptures applied to their current situation. Witnesses need to possess the same skill, and through daily Bible reading, their desire to be a daily witness will be enhanced.[28] A sanctifying effect of daily prayer and Bible study will be that they enable a person to become an effective witness. Vines instructs, "You witness by the consistency of your life, but you also witness by what you say with your lips."[29] Prayer and the study of Scriptures are essentials for a Christian to fulfill his responsibility to live and speak the Gospel.

Personal Evangelism Involves Winning and Growing. Vines asserts the secret of church growth, as found in Acts 2, is that the Spirit-filled experience of the disciples is not reserved for the pastor and staff alone, "It is for every one of us."[30] A church that is effective in winning people to Christ is comprised of a congregation of witnessing people. Acts 2:1-40 demonstrates that an important aspect of personal evangelism is sharing the Gospel for conversion growth, but that is only part of a witness' responsibility. According to Acts 2:41-47, a witness must also care for new converts by discipling them. Thus, personal evangelism entails both winning the lost and growing new Christians in their faith.

There are two paradigmatic insights that Vines incorporates into his teaching of evangelism from Acts 2. The first is that Peter's Pentecost sermon shows qualities of an effective Gospel presentation (2:1-40). The message should speak directly to the hearts of people and address the contemporary problems of the day. Its presentation is centered upon the Bible. Moreover, Jesus should be central to the message.[31]

A second paradigm for witnessing is discovered in the discipling of the new believers who were saved during Peter's Pentecost sermon (Acts 2:41-47). Following the picture of how the Jerusalem church cared for its new converts, Vines suggests six necessary steps for discipling new Christians:

Preach the Word!

1. Assurance of salvation is important to a new Christian. Satan cannot reclaim him, but he can rob him of needed assurance. A critical passage an expositor should use to teach assurance is 1 John 5:11-13.

2. New converts also need assurance of forgiveness. Too many new Christians somehow feel they must be perfect after they are saved. A discipler can turn to 1 John 1:9 to explain how a new believer deals with sins that he may commit.

3. Bible study is essential to spiritual growth. 1 Peter 2:2 compares the Word of God with milk for a new baby. New Christians will greatly benefit from being counseled by a discipler to begin reading the Gospel of John.

4. Next, share with a new Christian of the great opportunity of prayer. Ask him or her to consider how significant it is that believers can talk to the God of the universe. Show a new Christian Philippians 4:6-7 and help him or her understand prayer from that text.

5. Witnessing is a key to continued growth for Christians. Share with a new Christian Matthew 28:19-20. Talk to him about baptism being his first public witness for Christ. Also, encourage him to share his salvation experience with a family member or friend.

6. Finally, involvement in a local church is vital to being a growing Christian. Hebrews 10:24-25 underscores the importance of faithfulness to the church. Talk about the ministry of the local church and offer to bring the new believer to church.[32]

It is through winning and growing new believers that a church fulfills its responsibility in personal evangelism. These are not requirements of just the pastor and staff, for every believer is called to be a witness.

Every Christian Is to Engage in the Process of Cultivative Witnessing. In Acts 8:5-25, Luke writes of the witness of Philip, one of the original deacons of Acts 6, as he shared the Gospel in Samaria. Great joy is reported to have come to the city as a result of their acceptance of the Gospel. It is through Philip's example that Vines develops a principle of personal evangelism he calls "cultivative witnessing." He juxtaposes this passage with the account of Jesus' ministry in Samaria in John 4:1-42. Vines then reasons,

> Philip was merely one person in a process which had begun in Samaria previously. Philip was faithful to do his part. But he does not get sole credit for the phenomenal results. All the Lord wants us to do is sow the seed. The results are up to God. Thankfully, many who heard in Samaria were receptive to the Gospel. Along the way you will have opportunities to sow the seed in hearts that are receptive.[33]

He explains that not every witnessing encounter will result in immediate conversion, "One person begins the process. It is continued by others. It is completed by still others."[34] This lesson liberates a Christian from feelings of failure when he does not experience a harvest of new believers as a result of his evangelistic effort. He is to be a part of the process of scattering and sowing the seed of the Gospel, leaving the results to God.

Vines' teaching of cultivative witnessing has global implications. The geographical outline of Acts begins to unfold in the scattering of Acts 8. The Gospel is not bound to Jerusalem. It is now carried to Judea and Samaria. Later in Acts 13 it will be spread to the ends of the earth. Vines explains, "The fire is spreading. The river of God's grace is widening. God's program for evangelizing the world is moving out."[35] A Christian's life is guided by God's Divine providence. Jesus calls believers, in Matthew 13:38, the "good seed" who are sent throughout the world to spread the Gospel. As the witness obediently shares the Gospel in the location that God places him, the Gospel is disseminated throughout the world. These obedient witnesses, as they fulfill the Acts 1:8 commission, take part in "God's cultivative witnessing process."[36]

The Bible is the Indispensible Tool in Personal Evangelism. Philip's encounter with the Ethiopian eunuch offers another example of personal evangelism in Acts 8:26-40. This example follows the previous example of cultivative witnessing, for it offers an account of seed sown on receptive soil. The Holy Spirit led Philip into the path of the eunuch after he had sought

God in Jerusalem. Furthermore, Philip encounters the eunuch as he read from Isaiah 53. Philip's question asking if the man understood that which he was reading became his opportunity to explain that the passage of Scripture spoke of the Gospel about Jesus. Through Philip's obedience to follow the prompting of the Holy Spirit and explain the Scriptures, the eunuch trusted Christ as Savior.

Vines appeals to this text to teach of the need for every believer to follow the Holy Spirit's promptings for opportunities to witness. Yet the main application of the text is that like Philip, a witness must skillfully use the Bible as a tool in personal evangelism. "When the Word is sown in a human heart," Vines says, "Things happen."[37] Luke shows the importance of using the Word of God in witnessing, thus Vines does not wish to diminish the importance of one's personal testimony. Yet it is paramount that a Christian present God's plan of salvation as it is revealed in the Bible.

A Believer Must Confront Areas in His Life that Hinder His Witness. Peter's encounter with Cornelius in Acts 10:1-48 reveals how God works on both sides of a witnessing encounter when a person is saved. Vines describes the Centurion as a perfect prospect. Cornelius is a sincere seeker of God whom Luke describes as devout, God-fearing, generous, and faithful in prayer (2). Yet, he was not a Christian. Through an angel, God gave him a vision to send for Peter in Joppa.

Vines explains that God had more work to do in the heart of the evangelist than in the heart of an earnest God seeker:

> Peter, though a Christian and an apostle, needed to grow in several areas of his life. Many things must change in his heart before he could witness effectively. So often attitudes of the heart, hindrances in your lives, preconceived notions hinder your effectiveness for Jesus. As you shake your cities for Christ, God will have to remove some things from your lives.[38]

A hindrance to the effectiveness of Peter's witness was his prejudice. Vines asserts that the fear of failure can potentially yield similar, unwanted results.[39] To counter it, he appeals to Acts 10 to demonstrate that God has already gone before the witness before he engages in evangelism. Furthermore, a witness never fails when he gives a witness for Jesus. The only way to fail is for a believer to allow his hindrances to silence his witness. God works in many unbelievers' hearts much like he did in the heart of Cornelius. A Christian must overcome his hindrances in order to be obedient in personal evangelism.

What the Principles Teach Us

Vines' regular teaching and preaching through the book of Acts encoded the book into the very DNA of the churches he pastored. These principles, along with many others, offer timeless truths for personal evangelism that God has ordained for believers who are rightfully guided by the Bible's irresistible logic. This section considered matters related to the content of Vines' preaching and teaching that led the churches he pastored to persist in their evangelistic commitment. Even the particular mechanics of his preaching demonstrate his evangelistic focus.

Expository Preaching with an Evangelistic Twist

Vines has acquired the reputation of being both an expositor and an evangelistic preacher. He views these two elements of his preaching as inseparable and explains, "All Bible preaching issues forth into evangelism. Regardless of the Bible content of your message, the subject should include an evangelistic appeal."[40] The particular way he turns his sermons toward an evangelistic appeal is through what he calls "the evangelistic twist." He places it at the end of a sermon, and defines it as turning the message "toward an appeal to the unsaved in the audience to receive Jesus Christ as personal Lord and Savior."[41]

Underlying his use of "the twist" is the same irresistible logic that has been discussed repeatedly in this chapter. He reasons:

> I believe most of the Bible is written for believers. However, underlying all of Scripture and all expository preaching is a firm conviction I have about the rationale for evangelism: If there is a heaven, and there is; if there is a hell, and there is; then our greatest assignment is to tell people about Jesus, who died on the cross so people might not have to go to hell and can go to heaven.[42]

Every sermon gives Vines the opportunity to fulfill the evangelistic task that he determines to be a believer's greatest assignment. The evangelistic twist is a rhetorical tool he wields to faithfully fulfill this assignment. He uses it to transition his sermon from its Biblical subject to its Gospel invitation. It gives emphasis to the primary thrust of the passage as it twists the message toward evangelism. A survey of his pastoral preaching not only revealed that he consistently utilized the twist while remaining faithful to the text, but also, the variety of twists he employed demonstrate that it can be used in reproducible and sundry ways.

As an example of Vines' evangelist twist, consider his exposition of the creation account of Genesis 1:3-31. Vines presents his case that God created the world in a literal seven day, twenty-four hour week. He explains the details of the text and challenges his listeners that if they believe "in the beginning God," was powerful enough to create the world, they should also believe that God can perform His creative work in six days and rest on the seventh if He chooses. He then continues by expositing the fallacy of evolution. He rebuts theistic evolution and grounds Nietzsche's nihilism, Marxism, and Communism as social expressions of Darwinian thought. He discusses evolution's rejection of morality and explains that the more persons are told they are nothing more than animals, the more like animals they act. Then comes the twist:

> If I didn't know the Lord Jesus as my personal Savior, if I had not met God in the person of His Son, the Lord Jesus Christ, that verse right there would be one of the most frightening verses I had ever read in the Bible. The Bible says: It is appointed unto man once to die. You are going to die. When you are young, you think very little about death. When you get a little older you think a little bit more about death and the older you get the more and more you think about death. Someone said death is the subject that a man spends a lifetime trying not to think about. You are going to die. It is appointed unto man once to die. Your body will return to the earth from whence it was. That will not be the end of you. What does the evolutionist do with that? The evolutionist has no explanation for the existence and the origin of life, nor does he have any explanation for those characteristics which are beyond the realm of the physical. What does the evolutionist do with the

fact that down in your heart tonight you know when you die you will still be somewhere in eternity and you have to come face to face with God. God is unavoidable.[43]

The excerpt above is an example of an evangelistic twist that I classify as an "eternity twist."[44] The prospect of death, the judgment of God, and eternal consequence of sin are placed before his listeners. They are brought to a decision, and only the imputed righteousness of Christ will spare them from the consequences of their sin.

This evangelistic twist, an element of vintage Vines expository preaching, satisfies the irresistible logic of the Bible. It effectively twists the sermon but not its text. It meets the audience's need for a smooth transition into a Gospel appeal. It connects with the minds, wills, and hearts of the audience.

Conclusion

Presently, Southern Baptists in North America seem to be a long way from evangelistic effectiveness. In "A Resurgence Not Yet Realized: Evangelistic Effectiveness in the Southern Baptist Convention," Thom Rainer recollects that Southern Baptists were told that one of the primary benefits of the Conservative Resurgence "would be an unprecedented evangelistic harvest in the denomination."[45] Nevertheless, twenty-five years after the Resurgence began, Rainer's analysis of baptisms revealed that this promise had yet to be realized. He discovered that the North American churches of the Southern Baptist Convention were reaching no more people per year than they did in 1950. The Resurgence had not improved these baptismal trends, and the baptism figures since Rainer's article have not altered these conclusions.[46] These truths are heartbreaking. As much as ever before, Southern Baptists need ministers who live out resolute, undistracted evangelistic focus. Jerry Vines modeled this kind of focus. His years of pastoral ministry closely span the same years of Rainer's research, and his evangelistic focus yielded notable, trend-breaking results. From his ordination until his retirement as a pastor, the irresistible logic of the Bible kept him committed to doing the work of personal evangelism, training his church members to do the same, and preaching the Gospel from any Biblical text in a way that demanded a verdict. He is an example of a pastor who preached the Word, and did the work of an evangelist.

Growing a Church through Evangelistic, Biblical Preaching

by Steve Gaines

Some things naturally go together — a boy and a bicycle; a little girl and a doll; a cowboy and a horse, a referee and a whistle, and a politician and a smile. Preaching and evangelism are like that — they just logically go together.

Jesus certainly thought so. Our Lord was a preacher. "Jesus came ... preaching" (Mark 1:14). He Himself said, "I must preach the kingdom of God ... for I was sent for this purpose" (Luke 4:43). His primary purpose was not to heal the sick, feed the multitudes, or clothe the naked. Jesus came to preach the good news of God's kingdom. Through preaching, Jesus changed people's lives for both time and eternity.

After Jesus brought salvation to Zaccheus in the city of Jericho, He said, "The Son of Man has come to seek and to save that which was lost" (Luke 19:10). Not only had He come to preach; but He had also come to preach evangelistically. Jesus was God's first evangelistic preacher. He was both the message and the Messenger. Jesus was the Word of God (cp. John 1:1-2) who preached God's Word! That's why the guards said in John 7:46, "Never did a man speak the way" (Jesus spoke).

Every preacher should follow Jesus' example. A preacher should open his Bible and preach for the conversion of individuals. He should expect people to either accept or reject the Gospel every time he shares it. The sword of the Spirit is God's Word that divides humanity, forcing them into either belief or disbelief. The preacher literally stands between the sinner and eternity, offering him the gift of eternal life in Christ.

Since 1977, I have proclaimed the Gospel of Jesus Christ as a Baptist preacher. For most of those years I have been a pastor. I have served in all sizes of churches, ranging from small to very large. By God's grace, I have seen many people saved over the years.

Our church's Mission Statement is: "To Love God, Love People, share Jesus, and Make Disciples." I preach evangelistically to help accomplish these goals. More people are saved at a church that preaches the Gospel and gives an invitation to be saved than at a church that does not. If people come to church and never have an opportunity to hear the Gospel and be saved, a tragedy has occurred.

If the senior pastor is not evangelistic, the people will not be either. Unless the pastor preaches persuasively for a verdict, the church members will not be inclined to reach people for Christ. For a church to be on fire, the pulpit must be aflame.

To be sure, the Lord does the saving. We are allowed to plant and water the Gospel seed, but it is always the Lord who "causes the growth" (1 Corinthians 3:7). But God will not cause seeds that are not sown to grow. The seed will not leave the barn by itself, nor will it sow itself. The sower must go and sow the seed, which is the word of the Gospel (Mark 4:3,14).

Once the Gospel seed is sown, the sower must water that seed with love, tears, and fervent prayer. As the Psalmist said in Psalm 126:6, "He who goes to and fro weeping, carrying his bag of seed, shall indeed come again with a shout of joy, bringing his sheaves with him!" What a blessed partnership we have with the Giver of the Gospel seed!

Sadly, we live in a day when many books about preaching are written by people who have preached little, and served as a pastor even less. Oftentimes people with little or no real experience try to speak definitively and authoritatively regarding either preaching or evangelism (or both). The writings of such people are inherently limited. They are like the would-be automobile mechanic who had read many books about engines but had never actually worked on one. He really wanted to repair his neighbor's carburetor, but he just couldn't figure out how to get the hood of the car open!

The best books on preaching and evangelism come from preachers who have served extensively as senior pastors. There is simply no substitute for experience. Those who dabble in homiletical theories without ever having served "in the trenches" of the church should realize that it is easier to write about evangelistic preaching that leads to church growth than to do it.

The best teachers of preaching are veteran pastors who have written on the subject such as C. H. Spurgeon, D. Martin Lloyd Jones, John Stott, Stephen Olford, John MacArthur, and of course, Jerry Vines.

I have an earned Ph.D. from a Southern Baptist seminary with a major in Preaching and a minor in Evangelism. But more importantly, I have been preaching the Gospel evangelistically for over three decades. When it comes to evangelistic preaching that helps a church grow, I may not be an expert, but I am certainly not an armchair philosophizing novice. On thousands of occasions, in diverse settings, I have seen the Lord use evangelistic preaching to lead people to faith in Christ and grow His churches.

When it comes to Evangelistic Preaching, I am not a salesman; I'm a satisfied customer. I know it works! Like Paul, I am convinced that "God has chosen the foolishness of the message preached to save those who believe" (1 Corinthians 1:21).

What is evangelistic preaching? How should it be done? What are the essentials for a church that would endeavor to have worship services that honor Jesus Christ, help mature those who are saved, and also reach the lost for Christ?

America does not need more feel-good "communicators" who desire to merely dialogue with the culture and their congregations about vague, relative spiritual issues. G. Campbell Morgan said, "Sermonettes breed Christianettes."[1] Instead, we need "prophets." We need men who are God-called, Spirit-filled, Christ-honoring, Bible-believing preachers who will proclaim God's Word evangelistically.

What Is Evangelistic Preaching?

In order to grow a church through evangelistic, Biblical preaching, we need to comprehend the essence of evangelistic preaching. To do so we must first define both evangelism and preaching. I will give what I believe are the two best definitions for each of these terms. Regarding "evangelism," I submit the definition given by Dr. Roy Fish who served as Professor of Evangelism at Southwestern Baptist Theological Seminary for forty years. Dr. Fish describes evangelism as:

> The compassionate sharing of the good news of Jesus Christ in the power of the Holy Spirit with lost people for the purpose of winning them to Christ as Savior and Lord that they in turn may share Him also with others.[2]

Concerning "preaching," the classic definition in homiletical studies comes from Phillips Brooks who described preaching as, "The communication of truth by man to men. It has in it two essential elements, truth and personality."[3] Brooks believed that the "truth" that must be preached comes from the Bible and it should focus on the life and work of Christ. Scriptural truth concerning Christ captures the preacher's heart, and then he must share it with others.

As we review these two definitions, we see first of all that the *spirit* of evangelism should be one of compassion. We must love the people to whom we preach. If we do not, they will recognize our lack of genuine concern and disregard the Gospel we proclaim.

Dr. W. A. Criswell emphasized the fact that the preachers of the New Testament era were captured by both the passion wrought by their message and also the threatening condition and future destiny of their lost listeners.[4] They were concerned about the souls of the people to whom they preached! If you cannot weep for the soul of a lost man, you have no business trying to preach to him.

These definitions speak of the *message* of evangelistic preaching. We are to share "the good news of Jesus Christ." C. H. Spurgeon, who preached to thousands each week for almost forty years in the 1800s in London says,

> Let your sermons be full of Christ, from beginning to end crammed full of the gospel. As for myself, brethren, I cannot preach anything else but Christ and His cross, for I know nothing else, and long ago, like the apostle Paul, I determined not to know anything else save Jesus Christ and Him crucified ... Preach Jesus Christ, brethren, always and everywhere; and every time you preach be sure to have much of Jesus Christ in your sermon ... We preach Jesus Christ to those who want Him, and we also preach Him to those who do not want Him, and we keep on preaching Christ until we make them feel that they do want Him, and cannot do without Him.[5]

We are to speak Biblical "truth" concerning Jesus. Richard Armstrong emphasizes this by saying,

> In the most precise sense, evangelism is the proclamation of the Gospel. The word "evangel" is a transliteration of the Greek word *euaggelion*, translated *gospel*, which is a contraction of the Anglo-Saxon term *godspell*, meaning good tidings or good news. The New Testament evangel referred to either the good news that Jesus preached (the proclamation of the kingdom of God) or to the good news about Jesus, who was both the announcer and the revelation of the kingdom.[6]

Because it consists of good news, evangelistic preaching conveys a positive message. We must optimistically preach the Biblical message regarding Jesus. We should emphasize His virtuous life, His vicarious death, and His victorious resurrection. According to the Apostle Paul in 1 Corinthians 15:1-4, these are the essential facts that constitute the Gospel. Like Philip in Acts 8:35, we must open our mouths and preach Jesus to a lost world. What greater news could one man tell other men?

Our definitions tell us about the *power* of evangelistic preaching, which is "the Holy Spirit." The power of preaching comes from God's Spirit, not the intelligence and wisdom of the preacher. Paul said:

> And when I came to you, brethren, I did not come with superiority of speech or of wisdom, proclaiming to you the testimony of God. For I determined to know nothing among you except Jesus Christ, and Him crucified. I was with you in weakness and in fear and in much trembling, and my message and my preaching were not in persuasive words of wisdom, but in demonstration of the Spirit and of power, so that your faith would not rest on the wisdom of men, but on the power of God (1 Corinthians 2:1-5).

The Spirit alone is the One who convicts the sinner[7] and then converts him to Christ.[8]

These definitions also show that the *recipients* of evangelistic preaching are "lost people." God will sovereignly summon sinners to listen if the preacher will preach God's word evangelistically. Perry notes that there are usually four types of people in every congregation. These include, "believers … apathetic people, people with doubts, and usually some people who are hostile to the Gospel."[9] Some of those people are are in need of the saving Gospel we preach.

The *purpose* of evangelistic preaching is to "(win) them to Christ as Savior and Lord." When a preacher preaches evangelistically, he is not primarily concerned with addressing or meeting the social or material needs of mankind. Nor does he seek principally to instruct believers in righteousness. Instead, his goal is to proclaim Christ in such a way that non-Christians are brought under conviction and desire to be converted into faithful followers of Jesus Christ.[10] An evangelistic preacher simply seeks to lead the lost to Christ.[11]

The *perpetuation* of evangelistic preaching comes when "they (the new converts) in turn … share Him also with others." Once a person is saved, he should identify with a local church through baptism and membership. This is how churches "grow" in a Biblical sense. Unless people are saved, there is no legitimate "church growth." The new convert must then be trained to share the Gospel of Christ with others. Those won to Christ must seek to win others. While not all Christians will have a calling to be vocational evangelistic preachers, evangelism is the responsibility of every Christian. "All are to go, and to go to all."[12]

Our definitions speak of the *vehicle* of evangelism, which is the preacher. Evangelistic preaching involves "The communication of truth by man to men." God uses people to share the Gospel. Paul said in Romans 10:14, "How then will they call on Him in whom they have not believed? How will they believe in Him whom they have not heard? And how will they hear without a preacher?" As the message of salvation is proclaimed through the life and words of a preacher, some hearers will respond positively.

Preparing and Delivering an Evangelistic Sermon

I once read of an effective rural preacher who was trying to explain how he preached. He said, "I read myself full, pray myself hot, and then turn myself loose!"

If a church is going to grow by means of evangelistic, Biblical preaching, then the evangelistic preaching must come from a full head and a hot heart. If either is neglected, the preacher is ineffective and the listeners are cheated. Prayerless sermons lack power. When preachers do not study, the message lacks content. The former is like trying to shoot a bullet without gunpowder. The latter is like an empty gun with no bullet at all. Both miss the target!

Prayer and the Evangelistic Sermon

Preparing evangelistic sermons begins with prayer. Like Jesus, every preacher should rise early each day to spend time alone with God in prayer (Mark 1:35). Throughout the day he must pull aside to spend more time in prayer (Luke 5:16). A preacher who rarely talks *with* God has no business trying to talk *for* God. Prayer must become as natural for the preacher as breathing. We must pray for the Lord to open the meaning of every text of Scripture to us. As the Puritan preachers studied for their sermons, they would often pray, "More light, O Lord; more light!"

Prayer brings the power of God into our messages. The preacher should pray for the Lord to give him ideas from the Bible for soul-winning sermons. He should also pray for the Lord to help him interpret the text, craft appropriate illustrations, and determine sermonic application.

Prayer is a must for effective preaching. God uses our prayers to till the soil of the hearts of our listeners so that at least some of them will be receptive for the seed when it is sown and planted through our preaching.

Preparing for an Evangelistic Sermon

Prayer alone is not enough to make for good evangelistic preaching. Much "preaching" has just been "praying one's self hot" and "turning one's self loose" without also having "read one's self full." A preacher must not only pray; he must study God's word. He must "Be diligent to present (himself) approved to God as a workman who does not need to be ashamed, accurately handling the word of truth" (2 Timothy 2:15).

How to Secure a Sermon Idea

In preparing an evangelistic sermon, the preacher must first, immerse himself in the Biblical text. As he diligently and prayerfully reads, studies, and meditates upon the Scriptures, the Holy Spirit will cause the preacher to be drawn to a particular text. Soon a particular idea about that text will begin to surface in his mind and heart.

A preacher should get his sermon ideas from the Bible! He should not come up with a sermon idea and then try to find a text that fits his idea. Nor should he preach the sermons of other preachers. While not every Biblical text lends itself to evangelistic preaching, a conscientious preacher will not have trouble finding appropriate Biblical texts from which he can preach sermons that will be used to win souls.

Some excellent sources for evangelistic texts include the following:

Old Testament texts dealing with the great themes of God, man, sin, suffering, judgment and death.

Old Testament prophetic texts, particularly those given by God immediately prior to His judgment upon Israel and Judah by means of exiling them to foreign lands.

New Testament conversion experiences such as Zaccheus (Lk. 19), the Samaritan woman (John 4), the thief on the cross (Lk. 23), the Ethiopian eunuch (Acts 8), Saul/Paul (Acts 9), Cornelius (Acts 10), and the jailer at Philippi (Acts 16).

Events from the life of Jesus such as His virginal birth, sinless life, atoning death, bodily resurrection, and imminent return.

Doctrinal themes from the Bible such as God, Christ, sin, salvation, election, heaven, hell, the end of time, etc.

Specific Bible verses such as:
- Numbers 32:23 – "Your sin will find you out."
- 2 Kings 20:1 – "Set your house in order, for you shall die and not live."
- Isaiah 1:18 – "'Come now, and let us reason together,' says the LORD …"
- Daniel 5:27 – "'TEKEL' – you have been weighed on the scales and found deficient."
- Matthew 7:13-14 – "Enter through the narrow gate."
- Matthew 27:22 – "What shall I do with Jesus?"
- John 3:7 – "You must be born again."
- John 3:16 – "For God so loved the world …"
- Acts 3:19 – "Repent and return, so that your sins may be wiped away."
- Acts 16:30 – "What must I do to be saved?"
- Romans 5:1 – "Having been justified by faith, we have peace with God."
- Romans 6:23 – "The wages of sin is death, but the free gift of God is eternal life."
- Romans 10:13 – "Whoever calls on the name of the Lord will be saved."
- 2 Corinthians 5:17 – "If anyone is in Christ he is a new creature."

The "I Am" statements describing Jesus in John's Gospel:
- The Bread of Life (6:35)
- The Light of the World (8:12)
- I AM (8:58)

- The Door (10:9)
- The Good Shepherd (10:11, 14)
- The Resurrection and the Life (11:25)
- The Way, the Truth, and the Life (14:6)
- The True Vine (15:1).

Texts dealing with eschatological subjects such as:
- The Rapture of the Church (1 Corinthians 15:50-58; 1 Thessalonians 4:13-18)
- The Great Tribulation (Matthew 24:21; Revelation 6-19)
- The Return of Christ (Revelation 19:11-16)
- The Millennial Reign of Christ (Revelation 20:1-6)
- The Final Judgment (Revelation 20:7-15), and The New Jerusalem (Revelation 21-22).

Great "Invitations" from the Bible such as:
- Exodus 32:26 – "Who is on the Lord's side? Come to me!"
- Joshua 24:15 – "Choose today whom you will serve."
- 1 Kings 18:21 – "How long will you hesitate between two opinions? If the LORD is God, follow Him!"
- Mark 1:15 – "Repent and believe in the gospel."
- Matthew 4:19 – "Follow Me, and I will make you fishers of men."
- Matthew 11:28-30 – "Come to Me, all who are weary and heavy-laden."
- Acts 2:38 – "Repent and each of you be baptized."
- Acts 2:40 – "Be saved from this perverse generation!"
- Revelation 22:17 – "Come ... whosoever will."

For additional ideas concerning appropriate Biblical texts and themes for evangelistic preaching, you can consult Perry and Strubhar's excellent book, *Evangelistic Preaching*.[13]

Developing the Functional Elements of the Evangelistic Sermon

God is not the author of confusion; He loves order. The extent of structure can vary from a strict outline to a thematic approach. However it is developed, the evangelistic sermon should be well planned and thought-out. It should include some sort of introduction, explanation, illustration, application, and conclusion.

The Introduction

A sermon that begins poorly is in trouble. The first sentences of any sermon are critical. They are like the cry of an old time conductor calling for people to get on board the train that is about to pull out of the station.

The sermon introduction sets the stage for everything else that follows. The evangelistic preacher should keep his introduction brief. It should not be so wordy that the people are overwhelmed with excessive information. It should also be interesting. One of the best ways to make a sermon seem "shorter" is to make it more interesting! Charles Spurgeon once said, "Dull preachers make good martyrs. They are so dry they burn well."[14] "Boring preaching" is the preacher's fault, not the Bible's or the congregation's.

A good general format for an effective introduction is: (1) state the thesis sentence (central idea of the sermon); (2) share an illustration; (3) introduce the text (give the context as well as the burden of your message); (4) read the text; (5) announce the title; and (6) enter the body of the sermon.

Once the introduction is given, the preacher should explain, illustrate, and apply the Biblical text.

Explanation. Explanation deals with what the text meant in its original context and setting. The preacher must engage in an in-depth "historical, grammatical, and literary study of a passage in its context."[15] Explanation deals with the "then" part of the sermon and utilizes verbs in the past tense.

The preacher should avoid Biblical explanation that goes over the heads of his listeners. The average listener does not want a Greek lesson. Save that jargon for a theological lecture. Just explain the text in language that normal people can understand.

Illustration. It is good for the preacher to paint a memorable picture with carefully crafted words. Illustrations are like windows that allow additional light to shine on the meaning of the text.

The preacher must always be careful to use integrity in his illustrative material and avoid embellishing the facts. He should avoid telling sad stories that do not relate to the text just to move the emotions of his listeners. It is the Holy Spirit Who empowers preaching, not emotional exaggeration for the purpose of audience manipulation.

The best illustrations do not come from dated books of illustrations. It is better to give an illustration from personal experience, a Biblical incident, or from common occurrences in everyday life to which the majority of people can readily relate.

John Bisagno, who served as the pastor of First Baptist Church, Houston, Texas for thirty years, affirms this by saying,

> Ninety-five percent of the preachers I listen to are telling me stories from Scotland or England and France about Lord Chancellory, vicar of England, or Baron "Von Whosoever" of Scotland in the Seventeenth Century. Get rid of those old sermon illustration books and get into life. Read today's authors. Read modern books of sermon illustrations. Read *People, Time, Newsweek, USA Today,* and your local newspaper. Listen to the radio. Listen to television, particularly the evening news. Get among your people. Get out into the real world and find real, live, relevant illustrations.[16]

The listeners will seldom be able to recite your outline, but they will more than likely remember your stories and illustrations.

Application. Once the Biblical text has been explained and illustrated it needs to be applied. Some say that the preacher should merely explain the text and allow the Holy Spirit to take care of the application. The problem with that sort of reasoning is that it is simply not Biblical. Any study of the Old Testament prophets will confirm that they constantly applied the word that God had given them for His people. They did so with boldness, often using what some refer to as "the prophetic *you*." They did not say, "*We* need to repent." Rather they said, "*You* need to repent!" Jesus and the apostles used pointed application. They too use the prophetic "you." For years I have done the same and I know that God uses it to touch the hearts of people.

Whereas explanation deals with the "then" of the text, application addresses the "now." It utilizes present tense verbs. If I were applying John 3:7, I would say, "Just like Nicodemus, you need to be born again." The "you" is there, and the verbs are present tense and easy to understand.

Conclusion and Invitation. After the body of the sermon is completed, the listeners must be challenged to respond to what they have heard through the invitation. A great sermon can be basically nullified if the preacher does not know how to end well. The conclusion can briefly review the primary emphasis of the sermon body. This is also an excellent time to share an appropriate illustration. The sermon's primary theme can be restated. The primary portion of Scripture from which the message was derived can also be quoted again. At the end of the conclusion, the Gospel of Christ should be shared and an invitation to receive Christ should be given.

During the invitation of the sermon, the preacher should share about God's love for all, man's sin, Christ's death for man's sin, and man's need to repent from his sin and put his faith in Christ alone as Savior by accepting Him as Savior and Lord.

It is helpful for the preacher to have counselors available who can help lead those who want to be saved in the process of receiving Christ. Preachers who do not give their listeners the opportunity to be saved at the time the sermon is preached are guilty of a sin against both God and man. To delay is dangerous. That may be the last opportunity a person has to be saved. If they are not told how to be saved, encouraged to be saved, and given the opportunity to be saved, their blood is on the hands of an irresponsible preacher.[17]

I believe public invitations are important and Biblical. In our society, every ungodly person of every sort is proudly and publicly "coming out of the closet." It is time for Christ's followers to "come out of the closet" as well. Jesus died publicly for us. Is it too much for the preacher to ask converts to acknowledge Him before men? Billy Graham was fond of saying that everyone Jesus called, He called publicly. "Walking an isle" of a church does not save anyone. But a person who is genuinely converted to Christ should not refuse to acknowledge Jesus before his fellow man.

For an in-depth study of the public invitation, the reader is strongly encouraged to read the works of Roy Fish[18], O. S. Hawkins[19], R. Alan Streett[20], and Farris Whitesell.[21]

There needs to be a smooth transition in the conclusion to the invitation. I believe the invitation is the most important time of the worship experience. No one should leave the sanctuary during that critical moment. The least distraction can be a tool of Satan to disrupt and break the concentration of a lost sinner who is contemplating being saved.

Likewise, a preacher should never shut his Bible just before he extends the invitation. Closing one's Bible sends the message that the important part of the sermon is over.

The preacher should give the invitation compassionately, confidently, cheerfully, and concisely. Tell the people exactly what they are to do. Say, "If today you desire to repent of your sin, believe in and receive Christ, as soon as the worship music begins, come forward and take one of the pastors by the hand. If you have been saved but have not yet been baptized, come and obey Christ's command in that crucial area. If you would like to join our church, come and do so the moment we begin to sing our hymn of surrender and commitment." Notice how clear these invitational instructions are. Notice also how often the word "come" is used. It is a powerful word because it is a Biblical word (Revelation 22:17) that God Himself uses to draw people to salvation![22]

An evangelistic preacher must take every precaution to avoid manipulative tactics throughout his sermon, especially during the invitation. Most of us have cringed as we have witnessed preachers using their "tricks" to get people to come forward. A lost person needs to be guided, not beguiled. So-called "decisions" that come from exploiting people's emotions do more harm than good because they were prompted by "cleverness of speech"[23] rather than the conviction of God's Spirit. A preacher simply needs to share the truth of the Gospel, and then lovingly and articulately invite men to receive Christ as Savior.

Conclusion

It is a wonderful privilege and responsibility it is to preach the Gospel of Jesus Christ so that people will be saved and churches will grow. Stephen Olford emphatically affirmed this by stating, "God has chosen people like you and me to be preachers of the Gospel. The awesomeness of this calling is almost overwhelming when we realize that God had only one Son, and He made Him a preacher."[24] The British Methodist preacher, W. E. Sangster concurs by saying,

> Called to preach! ... Commissioned of God to teach the Word! A herald of the great King! A witness of the eternal Gospel! Could any work be more high and holy? To this supreme task God sent His only begotten Son. In all the frustration and confusion of the times, is it possible to imagine a work comparable in importance with that of proclaiming the will of God to wayward men?[25]

The need of the hour is for churches that will grow through evangelistic, Biblical preaching. Prayer must permeate both the development and the delivery of the evangelistic sermon. The preacher must study the Biblical text in such a way that his head is full, and then pray and worship God fervently so that his heart will be ablaze. He must also live a life of moral integrity so that His message will be believable. He should not mince words. Rather, he should boldly and compassionately "speak the truth in love."[26]

If a preacher should be able to do anything, he ought to be able to preach. If he preaches, he ought to preach evangelistically so the Lord will be glorified and His church will grow. I pray that our Lord will graciously grant us a revival of evangelistic preachers and preaching. If we will "read ourselves full, pray ourselves hot, and turn ourselves loose," God will bless, souls will be saved, saints will be edified, churches will prosper, and Christ will be honored.

Part V:
The Preacher Preaching

Jerry Vines

A Word from the Late Dr. Adrian Rogers on the Preaching of Jerry Vines

*T*his message by Jerry Vines, "A Baptist and His Bible," is a wonderful example of scholarship, conviction, and truth presented from a heart on fire and a heart in love with Jesus and His Word.

I had the joy of presiding over the meeting of the Southern Baptist Convention in June 1987 in St. Louis, Missouri, when this dynamic sermon was first preached. Sitting where I was on the platform, I could sense the impact it was having on the hearers. The sermon was punctuated with "amens," applauses, and even standing ovations. It was very obvious that Dr. Vines was causing sympathetic vibrations in the hearts and lives of people to whom the Word of God is precious.

My own heart was deeply stirred to have affirmed one more time that the rank and file of Southern Baptists are people of The Book. We may be diverse in many ways, but real Baptists are united in the Word of the Lord and the Lord of that Word.

You, dear reader, will be informed, encouraged, and fortified by this timely message on God's timeless Word. May God bless it to your heart.

> Dr. Adrian Rogers
> Southern Baptist Convention
> President 1987-88

A Baptist and His Bible

by Dr. Jerry Vines

II Timothy 3:14–4:13

In beautiful human language resplendent with Divine revelation Paul sets before us the Bible's doctrine concerning itself. He quickly takes us to the Counseling Room and shows us the intention of the Bible; the Class Room and shows us the inspiration of the Bible; then the Crisis Room and shows us the implications of the Bible.

I am interested that Paul refers to the Bible as "the Holy Scriptures." The word combination is unusual, found only here in the New Testament: *ta hiera grammata*. Paul normally uses the word *graphe* (Scriptures) as in verse 16 or *ho logos* (the word) as in 4:2. But here he uses *grammata* which sometimes refers to the letters of the words themselves or to the document. The word for holy is also unusual. Not the normal *hagios* but *hiera*. This word is found only one other time. In I Corinthians 9:13 reference is made to the *sacred things of the temple*. The sacred things were the utensils set apart for God in temple services. The word means sacred or pertaining to God. Only of the Bible can it be said that it is the Sacred Scriptures. The Bible is the only book set apart for God's special use. This term attaches great reverence to the Bible.

"The Holy Scriptures." Paul sounds like a Baptist! A Presbyterian, a Pentecostal, and a Baptist preacher were discussing what denomination Paul would join should he return to earth. The Presbyterian said, "I am sure he would join the Presbyterians. He would love our scholarship." The Pentecostal said, "Oh, no, he would be a Pentecostal, praise God! Read his doxologies." The Baptist preacher replied, "Oh, I don't think he would change!"

"The Holy Scriptures." That is Baptist talk. Wherever you find a Baptist, somewhere nearby you will find a Bible. That Baptist will speak with respectful tones of the Bible in his hands. Baptists are early taught to love and respect the Bible. On a hot summer day at Vacation Bible School, little Baptist feet carry little Baptist bodies into the awesome church auditorium. Billy Baptist stands before his little classmates and with trembling hands holds a Bible. Little Baptist voices sing, "Holy Bible, Book divine, precious treasure, thou art mine." Baptists are known as a people of The Book. We are a Bible-reading, Bible-believing, Bible-loving, and Bible-sharing people.

With Paul's words to young Timothy to guide us, think with me for a while about a Baptist and his Bible. First, he takes us into the Counseling Room and shows us:

I. The INTENTION of the Bible (3:14-15)

But continue thou in the things which thou hast learned ...

That's continuation. The Bible is intended to help us live consistent Christian lives, moving to maturity ... *the things which thou hast learned and hast been assured of ...* That's conviction. The Bible is intended to place our lives on a firm, assured foundation. *And that from a child thou has known the Holy Scriptures, which are able to make thee wise unto salvation ...* That's conversion. The Bible is primarily intended to bring people to salvation.

That's what the Bible did for young Timothy. When I was a boy most Baptist churches had a TEL Class named for Timothy, Eunice, and Lois. His was a heritage of faith. Each day his godly mother, Eunice, and his godly grandmother, Lois, would take the sacred Scriptures and prepare the day's Bible lesson for Timothy. "What Bible lesson shall we teach tiny Tim today?" They were preparing his little heart. Then one day Paul preached at First Baptist Church, Lystra. At the invitation time down the aisle came Timothy.

He gave his hand to Paul and his heart to Jesus. What a testimony was his—from his mother's knee to his Master's knee! I can imagine a deacon went home that day and someone asked, "Did anything happen at church today?" "Not much. We had a long-winded preacher. Oh, yes, Eunice's boy, Timothy, joined the church. Not much." Not much? Paul's traveling companion was converted. Not much? The recipient of two Bible letters was born again. Not much? The angels in heaven were rejoicing because another sinner was converted.

That's what the Bible is intended to do—to make wise unto salvation. To know the Bible is not synonymous with salvation, but it does point us to the One who can save us. This is why Psalm 19:7 says, *The law of the Lord is perfect, converting the soul.* And John 20:31 says, *But these are written, that ye might believe that Jesus is the Christ, the Son of God; and that believing ye might have life though His name.* The vehicle of the Written Word brings us to the Living Word and thus to salvation.

Wise unto salvation. How smart do I have to be to be saved? First, I have to know I am a great sinner. The Bible confirms what experience screams in my soul. *All have sinned and come short of the glory of God* (Romans 3:23). Mary Baker Eddy claimed that her book, *Science, Health and the Scriptures*, could cure appendicitis. I don't know about that, but this book can cure "devilitis!"

Second, I have to know that God has provided a great Savior. The Bible points to Jesus. He is the central theme of the Bible. Acts 10:43 says, *To Him give all the prophets witness ...* The Old Testament predicts Him; the New Testament presents Him. The Old Testament anticipates Him; the New Testament announces Him. If you want to know about the stars, read a book on astronomy. If you want to know about the Bright and Morning Star, read the Bible. If you want to know about the ages of the rocks, read geology; if you want to know about the Rock of Ages, read the Bible. If you want to know about the roses and the lilies of the fields, read botany; if you want to know about the Rose of Sharon and the Lily of the Valley, read the Bible.

I find my Lord in the Bible,

Wherever I choose to look.

He is the theme of the Bible,

The center and heart of The Book.

He is the Rose of Sharon,

He is the Lily fair.

Wherever I open my Bible,

The Lord of The Book is there.

This is why Acts 4:12 says, *Neither is there salvation in any other; for there is none other name under heaven given among men, whereby we must be saved.*

What other book can change lives? Did you ever hear a man say, "I was a thief. One day I read a math book and it really straightened me out"? Or, "I was impure, I read in a geometry book, and it surely cleaned me up"? Or, "I was a liar. I read a book on anatomy and I have been telling the truth ever since"? Or, "I was a drunk. I read a chemistry book and it sobered me up"? But I can take you places where I have preached this Book and show you drunkards made sober, liars made truthful, and adulterers made pure. James 1:21 says, *Receive with meekness the engrafted word, which is able to save your souls.* There is no debate here. We all understand what the Bible is intended to do.

Because we understand the Bible's intention, Baptists get concerned when there is any hint of attack upon it. We get upset when there is any undermining of its authority, questioning of its reliability, or denying of its accuracy. This Book has to do with man's eternal destiny. To attack the Bible is like tampering with medicine for a sick man, like poisoning the bread of a hungry man.

The noted preacher, Henry Ward Beecher, was invited to be the guest of an Atheist Club presided over by Robert Ingersoll, the noted infidel. He went and listened to a brilliant speech by Ingersoll, who attacked Christianity unmercifully. Ingersoll sat down amidst thunderous applause. He turned to Beecher and invited him to say a few words in defense of the Bible. Beecher rose slowly to his feet: "Gentlemen, forgive me if I seem a bit shaken. I saw something shocking on the way to the meeting. I saw a poor, blind man with a cane, groping at the curbside. A young lad came along, offering to help him across the street. As he took the blind man's arm a hulk of a man came along, bullied the boy, broke the blind man's cane, pushed the blind man in the mud, and went on his way laughing." A silence fell over the meeting. Then Ingersoll leaped to his feet, eyes blazing, "The bully," he roared, "Do you know who he is, Beecher?" "Yes, I know who he is. It is you! Mankind is poor, blind, and wretched. He has little enough to lean on as it is and few to help him on his way. What do you do, Ingersoll? You come along, break his faith in the Bible, push him in the mud, and go on your way laughing. I tell you, Ingersoll, you are the man!"

How can anyone say we must trust our soul to Christ for eternity, then turn around and try to obliterate the very document which tells us about Him? We honor the Book and earnestly contend for it because we know what it is intended to do.

Next, Paul takes us to the Class Room and shows us:

II. The INSPIRATION of the Bible (3:16-17)

For a while we are going to step into the Class Room. I am so thankful to God for the men who taught me during my seminary days. I am grateful for Dr. Gray Allison who instilled in my heart a burning desire to win the lost to Christ. I will never forget the day Dr. George Harrison showed me the beauty of Christ in the tabernacle. I left his classroom with glory in my soul. I shall never forget the week Dr. J. Wash Watts spent meticulously dismantling the documentary hypothesis. At the conclusion of the week, this godly professor, with tears in his eyes, raised his Bible above his head and said, "Young men, the documentary hypothesis makes your Bible nothing more than a scrapbook!" I wish every young man called to preach could sit in classrooms with teachers such as these.

I return to the Class Room again. Not as a scholar, but as a student. Not as a teacher, but as a learner. I am trying to understand the inspiration of my Bible. What I am after is what someone has called a "simple Biblicism."

With breathtaking brevity of language, Paul says, *All Scripture is given by inspiration of God*. Actually he uses only three words in the original text: *pasa*, *graphe*, and *theopneustos*. The last of these words, *theopneustos*, is translated by five words in the King James, *given by inspiration of God*. This is actually one compound Greek word, coming from *theos (*God) and *pneo* (to breathe). The word seems to have been coined by the Holy Spirit to give us a glimpse into the mystery of inspiration. The word is a verbal adjective used in a passive sense. The emphasis is that God alone is the agent in the Bible's inspiration. The Bible is the product of the creative breath of God. "God-breathed." That's the best way to translate it. Not man-breathed; God-breathed.

A. God-breathed.

This means SUPERNATURAL inspiration.

All Scripture is God-breathed. The Bible owes its origin and contents to the Divine breath of God. In creation God picked up the lifeless clay that was Adam, *breathed into his nostrils the breath of life, and man became a living* soul (Genesis 2:7). In inspiration, God picked up the lifeless pages of man's composition and the Bible became a living book. Hebrews 4:12 (RSV) says, *For the Word of God is living* ... This book pulsates with life. It breathes, bleeds, sings and weeps. Charles H. Spurgeon said, "If you cut this book into a thousand pieces, every part would grow and live." Just as a little child puts a seashell to its ear and can hear the blowing of the waves in the sea, so we with childlike faith hear the breath of God blowing through the pages of the Bible.

Supernatural inspiration doesn't eliminate the human element in the Bible. The personalities of the human authors are everywhere apparent. We see the burning sarcasm of Isaiah. We witness the moving pathos of Jeremiah, the deep philosophy of John, and the crisp logic of Paul. Amos writes like a farmer, Simon Peter like a fisherman. Luke writes like a doctor, James like a preacher. Each writer was sovereignly prepared by the Holy Spirit to be the ideal penman for that portion of Scripture. Does God want a selection of Psalms like David's? He prepares a David to write them! Does He want a series of letters like Paul's? He prepares a Paul to write them!

Human authorship must never be separated from the Divine inspiration of the Bible. The human aspect is only one aspect under the category of its divine character. Actually there is a dual authorship in the Bible. Second Peter 1:21 says, ... *Holy men of God spoke* ... Yes, but, *as they were moved* (borne along) *by the Holy Spirit*. Like a vessel gently carried along by the wind, so the Holy Spirit was the guiding, moving force in the Bible's composition. Acts 1:16 makes this dual authorship very plain, *This Scripture must needs have been fulfilled which the Holy Spirit by the mouth of David spake.* The Holy Spirit is speaking in Scripture. He speaks by the mouth of David.

The tendency today in much scholarship is to so emphasize the human authorship of the Bible that the Divine is minimized. We are told that since the Bible is touched by fallible, error-prone men, it must be fallible and prone to err. The logic doesn't follow. If God can overcome man's tendency to err at one point, why not at every point? The Divine human nature of the Bible is analogous to the Divine human nature of Christ. Christ was fully God and fully man, yet, without sin. He was touched by our humanity, but not tainted by our depravity. The Bible was given by men superintended by the Holy Spirit so that what they wrote was without error. *God breathed.* God does not breathe error.

Others tell us that the Bible is accurate on salvation matters but not on matters of science or history. Obviously, the Bible is not a science book. But, when it touches on science, it does so truthfully. Neither is the Bible a history book. But, its historical statements are reliable. If you can't believe what the Bible says about the creation, how can you believe what it says about salvation? If you can't trust it concerning history, how can you trust it concerning eternity? We would do well to ponder the words of Jesus, *If I have told you earthly things, and you believe not, how shall ye believe, if I tell you of heavenly things?* (John 3:12). Take, for example, a physics book. A physics book is not a math book. However, there are mathematical statements in it. If I constantly find mathematical errors in the physics text, how can I trust its statements concerning physics?

Further, how do we separate salvation matters from other matters? Take the virgin birth. If the virgin birth is not historical and biological fact, then it is theological fiction. Or consider the resurrection of Christ. If there was not a time when and a place where the resurrection occurred, what kind of resurrection was it? Salvation matters are so embedded in historical matters that you cannot consistently attribute inspiration to the one and deny it to the other. Every line, every sentence, every word, and every letter was placed in our Bible by the supernatural inspiration of God.

B. God-breathed.

This means VERBAL inspiration.

All Scripture is God-breathed. The word is *graphe*, meaning from *grapho*, to write. The obvious reference is to the words. The words of the Bible are God-breathed. Some tell us that the words are not necessarily inspired, but only the thoughts. I am no scholar, but no one has ever explained to me how it is possible to have thoughts without words. Try it sometime. Think a thought without words. What kind of thought did you think? Were no words involved?

Words are vehicles of thought. I heard about two Indians talking. The first one said, "Ugh." The second one replied, "Ugh." The first one said, "Ugh." The second replied, "Ugh, ugh." The first one said, "Don't change the subject!"

Remove the words from the page and the thoughts disappear. There can be no music without notes; no math without numbers; no geology without rocks; no thoughts without words. First Corinthians 2:13 sets forth the verbal inspiration of the Bible, *Which things we also speak, not in the words which man's wisdom teaches, but which* (words) *the Holy Spirit teaches.* Where do you find words the Holy Spirit teaches? In the Bible.

Did Jesus teach verbal inspiration? You decide. *Man shall not live by bread alone, but by every word that proceeds out of the mouth of God* (Matthew 4:4). Not some of the words, nor part of the words, but every word. *Heaven and earth shall pass away, but My words shall not pass away* (Matthew 24:35).

Jesus goes further than that. Matthew 5:18 is the strongest statement about inspiration ever made. He begins by saying, *verily*. This is a strong word of affirmation. Then He says that not *one jot* will pass from the law. A jot is the smallest letter in the Hebrew alphabet. It is merely a breath mark, the stroke of a pen. Nor *one tittle* shall pass away. A tittle is a little horn on a Hebrew letter. It is only about 1/32nd of an inch. Don't forget your tittle! You can change a Hebrew letter by its omission. When I was taking Hebrew I tried to keep flies off my test paper. I might mistake a fly's leg for a tittle and flunk the test! Jesus also said, *In no wise shall pass from the law.* Actually a double negative is used here for emphasis. You could read the statement this way, "Under no circumstances, never." Now, let's put it all together. Jesus said, *Until heaven and earth pass away the smallest letter of the Hebrew alphabet and the smallest part of a letter shall under no circumstance ever pass from the law till all be fulfilled.* Such is our Lord's view of inspiration.

We love the words of the Bible: salvation, justification, sanctification, faith, love, hope. "Sing them over again to me, wonderful words of life. Let me more of their beauty see, wonderful words of life."

C. God-breathed.

This means TOTAL inspiration.

All Scripture is God-breathed. Pasa. Dr. Herschel Hobbs has given the best explanation of the meaning of the word *pasa* I have read. He says, "It means that every single part of the whole is God-breathed." That's where I stand. That's where Southern Baptists have always stood. Jed and his wife were riding in the pick-up to town on a Saturday morning. His wife turned to him and said, "Jed, when we first married, we didn't sit this far apart." Jed looked up and said, "I ain't moved." I'm standing where Southern Baptists have always stood. When Southern Baptists stand where they should be standing, they'll be standing where I'm standing! We affirm total inspiration.

At the turn of the century an old thief quietly entered the country. He had already robbed Germany of spiritual authority and moral conscience. He first appeared in the Garden of Eden, calling into question the authorship, accuracy, and acceptability of God's Word. This old thief began entering and robbing in the North, leaving a trail of stripped denominations, faith-depleted schools, and powerless churches.

He moved steadily down the eastern coast. A very crafty thief, he appealed to man's intellectual pride. His goal? To snatch the Bible from the man in the pew. He travels under many aliases. I want to unmask him. The name of the old thief is Destructive Criticism. Not reverent, believing scholarship, but destructive, faith-wrecking criticism. That criticism which clips faith's wings with reason's scissors. That kind of destructive scholarship which submits the warm wonder of the Word to the cold, merciless analysis of unbelief.

This old thief is a demolition expert. He has many tools in his tool chest. None are constructive; all are destructive. He has a heretical hammer, driving into the Bible the nails of anti-supernaturalism and anti-miraculous. He explains away every account of miracle as natural phenomena or primitive folklore. He has a critical saw, dividing Scripture and the Word of God. He puts asunder what God has joined together. According to the old thief some of the Bible is, some isn't, the Word of God. The Bible is only inspired in spots. Only those who use his tools can tell you which spots are the inspired spots! He also has a cynical crowbar, ripping the Bible from the hands and hearts of simple believers.

But, old thief, your tools are fatally flawed. Your heretical hammer won't do. To reject the miraculous and supernatural in the Bible is to deny the Bible its own nature. You can't kick God out of His Book anymore than you can kick Him out of His universe. I believe in the miracles of the Bible. I really believe Jonah was swallowed by a great fish. How the fish stood him, I don't know, but I believe it. I do believe Daniel survived a night in the lion's den. He had a lion's mane for a pillow and used its tail to swish away mosquitoes. Early the next morning the frantic king called, "Daniel, are you there?" "Yes, what's for breakfast?"

I don't have all the answers to all the difficulties in the Bible. I can't place my peanut brain alongside God's infinite mind and not expect to have some problems. But, my list of difficulties has been progressively getting smaller. When I run across a difficulty in the Bible, I do not suppose the error is in the text, but rather in my understanding. "Where did Cain get his wife?" I don't know and I don't care. If she suited Cain, she suits me. I don't understand all the Bible, but I believe it all. I believe it all from Genesis to Maps!

Old thief, your cynical saw is dull. You can't separate the Word of God from Scripture. Note that Paul uses Scriptures (3:15), Scripture (3:16), and the Word (4:22) interchangeably in this passage. When Scripture speaks— God speaks. Jesus said, *Thy word is truth* (John 17:17). Not, contains truth, but is truth. When you try to separate the Word of God from Scripture, there is no stopping place. The Bible cannot be put on trial every few days while theologians hold symposiums to pool their ignorance.

When you force the Bible to pay tribute at every little "toll gate" of rational opinion, eventually you give away every part of the Bible. You begin by giving up the Genesis account of creation; next you dissect the historical parts of the Bible; then the miracles have to go. Before it is over you are picking and choosing from the very words of Jesus. Perhaps you have heard about the Jesus Seminar. This group of scholars is planning to put out a color-coded New Testament. The intention is to show us which of the words in the New Testament were actually the words of Jesus and which were put in His mouth by the church. Have you heard about the garbage barge in the Atlantic? I would suggest this color-coded New Testament be put on the garbage barge so all who purchase it will recognize it for the garbage it is. When you start trying to separate the Word from Scripture, you wind up with a fictitious creation, three Isaiahs, exaggerated miracles and a speechless Jesus. Before it is over, you have a Bible full of holes instead of a whole Bible!

Old thief, your critical crowbar won't do. This is the most serious flaw of all. Only the so-called critical scholars are supposed to be qualified to explain what the Bible means. At the Inerrancy Conference in Ridgecrest in May 1987, Clark Pinnock was quoted as saying to reporters, "Adrian Rogers does not really know the Bible and Roy Honeycutt does. How do you deal with people who don't know the Bible?" (*Florida Baptist Witness*, June 1987). Let me say, first of all, I do not believe Roy Honeycutt would ever say that. He is too much a gentleman. Further, I don't think Dr. Honeycutt would believe that. Poor Adrian Rogers. He doesn't have to be a Bible ignoramus all his life. Why doesn't he subscribe to my "tape of the month" plan! Look carefully at what is suggested in Pinnock's statement. The preacher doesn't know the Bible; the professor does. The two are pitted against each other. Do you know what that sounds like to me? The priesthood of the scholar. Baptists affirm the priesthood of the believer. We do not believe our preachers and professors should be pitted against each other, but be in partnership with one another, helping us find out what God has said in the Bible. That's the Baptist way and I like it!

We believe the Bible was given for common men. The Holy Spirit can take an unlettered man and give him amazing insight into the Bible. One of the greatest Bible students I ever knew was a man named Ed Shellhorse. Ed never owned a car until he retired. He worked all his life in a fabric mill. He read the Bible many hours each night after work. His insight into the

Scriptures was amazing. The same Holy Spirit who inspired common men to write the Bible can illuminate common men to understand it.

I must make a choice. On one side is the old thief, destructive criticism. On the other side is the infallible Son of the Living God. What about the stated authors of Bible books? For instance, Moses and the Pentateuch? The old thief says Moses could not possibly have written it, because writing was unknown in that day. The Lord Jesus says, *For had ye believed Moses, ye would have believed Me: for he wrote of Me. But if you believe not his writings how shall ye believe My words?* (John 5:46-47).

Were Adam and Eve really persons? The old thief says they were merely representative and never existed in fact. The Lord Jesus says, *Have ye not read, that He which made them at the beginning made them male and female?* (Matthew 19:4).

Did the miracles of the Bible actually occur? For instance, the ark and the flood? The old thief says this was merely a local legend which found its way into the Bible. The Lord Jesus says, *They were given in marriage, until the day that Noah entered into the ark, and the flood came and destroyed them all* (Luke 17:27). Is the Bible totally inspired? The old thief says only the salvation parts. The Lord Jesus says, *O fools, and slow of heart to believe all that the prophets have spoken:* (I didn't say it, Jesus did. If you don't believe all the prophets said, you have a head and a heart problem) *and beginning at Moses and all the prophets, He expounded unto them in all the Scripture the things concerning Himself.* Jesus affirms every major section of the Old Testament. He quotes from the first chapter of Genesis and the last chapter of Malachi. Virtually everything the old thief denies Jesus affirms. When you read the words of Jesus, it's as if He anticipated every modern attack against the Bible. At no time did He ever raise the slightest suspicion concerning the Scriptures.

The matter of the total inspiration of the Bible must be decided on the basis of lordship, not scholarship. I do not mean by this that it is unscholarly to believe in total inspiration.

Robert Dick Wilson was professor of Semitic languages at Princeton Theological Seminary. He was considered the greatest Biblical linguist of modern times. To answer the destructive critics he learned all the cognate languages of the Bible and all the languages in which the critics had written. He learned Hebrew, Greek, Aramaic, French, German, Latin, Egyptian, Coptic, and Syrian. He made himself at home in 45 languages and dialects. To answer a single sentence of a noted critic, he read all the extant ancient literature of the period under discussion in numerous languages. He collated no less than 100,000 citations. From the material he got at the basic facts, which when known, proved the critic was wrong! Critics then and now can't handle him. This is what he said, "After 45 years of scholarly research and Biblical textual studies and language study, I have come to the conclusion that no man knows enough to assail the truthfulness of the Old Testament" (*Knights Illustrations for Today*, page 22). Yet, I repeat, ultimately the question of total inspiration must be decided on the basis of lordship, not scholarship. The decision must be one of the heart, not of the head.

I don't know about you, but I have heard enough from the old thief. I feel like the dear old grandmother who couldn't hear well. Her grandchildren insisted she go to the doctor. The doctor said, "I can solve your problem. All you need is a minor operation and you'll hear fine." Grandmother said, "There'll be no operation. I'm seventy-nine years old and I've heard enough!" I will study my Bible with more reverent, faith-building methods. I will study it textually, historically, grammatically, contextually, theologically, and practically. I will study it on the basis of a "simple Biblicism" which never calls into question the supernatural, verbal, or total inspiration of the Bible. Let the critics pick over the bones of the Bible. Bible-believing Baptists will continue to feast on the meat of the Word.

Finally, Paul takes us to the Crisis Room and shows us:

III. The IMPLICATIONS of the Bible (4:1-13)

What one believes about the Bible's intention and inspiration has certain implications. From these verses in chapter four let me mention just a few of these implications. The Bible has:

Preach the Word!

A. EXPOSITIONAL Implications (4:1-4)

Preach the Word, says Paul. Preach it faithfully, as a herald declares the message of his king; preach it incessantly, in season and out of season; preach it effectively, reprove, rebuke, exhort; preach it persistently, even though men might not endure sound doctrine.

Preaching is central in the worship of Baptist churches. Go into the average Baptist church on Sunday and you will find a pulpit in the middle. Chances are you will find a Baptist preacher standing with a Bible in his hand, preaching from the top of his head, the bottom of his heart, and probably to the top of his lungs! I really believe there is no preaching like Southern Baptist preaching. The best preachers in America are in the pulpits of our Southern Baptist churches. Did you hear about the Southern Baptist preacher having coffee with his wife on a Monday morning? He was feeling good about his sermons the previous day. He leaned back and with a sigh said, "You know, there are only a few great preachers left." "Yes," his wife replied, "and there is one less than you think there is."

What the preacher believes about the Bible is crucial to the task of exposition. A low view of inspiration erodes the very foundation of preaching. Decide the Bible is not totally the Word of God and there will be no responsibility to study its text minutely and to preach its message authoritatively. Our most famous Southern Baptist evangelist, Billy Graham, punctuates his sermons with the now well-known phrase "the Bible says." Obviously, the source of his authority and power is "thus saith the Lord."

I was interested to read again the account of the building of Solomon's temple. The whole thing went up without a fuss. Wouldn't you like to see Baptist churches build something without a fuss? The stones, hewed underground, fit exactly. When the temple was dedicated, hundreds of animals were sacrificed. A great white-robed choir and a magnificent orchestra performed. When it was all done, they took the old Ark of the Covenant and put it in the Holy of Holies of the new temple. They stayed with the old ark. We don't need a new Bible. My preacher brother, preach the old Book; it will do the job. I think of so many dear people who go to church hungry and are given only bones to gnaw. People want to hear again the old, old truths from the old, old Book.

Though its cover is worn,

And its pages are torn,

And though places bear traces of tears.

Yet, more precious than gold,

Is this Book worn and old

That can shatter and scatter our fears.

Preacher man, I'm going to hit you with a hard lick. A sweet Quaker brother found a burglar in his home. There the burglar stood, arms full of stuff, ready to run. The Quaker cocked both triggers of his double-barreled gun and said, "I would not hurt thee for any thing, but I'm about to shoot where thou standest!" I'm getting ready to shoot where you stand. If you don't believe the Bible, don't take a salary for preaching it. If you don't believe the Bible, do the world a favor and get a milk route. You will do more good. Our people come in on Sunday from a world of cynicism and doubt and unbelief. They have enough question marks in their lives; what they need are some exclamation points!

My days in college were great days. However, I had to make a decision about some of the things I was hearing concerning the Bible. I knew I would never be as scholarly or smart as those professors who were questioning the authority of the Bible. Thirty-one years ago now, as an eighteen year old boy, I decided to accept the Bible by faith and try to preach it. For me, the proof of the pudding is in the eating. I know the Bible is the Word of God.

I know the Bible was sent from God,

The old as well as the new.

Divinely inspired the whole way through,

I know the Bible is true.

The Bible has:

B. EVANGELISTIC Implications (4:5)

Paul says, *Do the work of an evangelist*. Not all have the gift of the evangelist, but all should do the work of evangelism. Evangelism and missions are at the heart of all Southern Baptists do. Southern Baptists became great because of preachers and missionaries and evangelists and denominational leaders and lay people who carried New Testaments into the homes of lost people and led them to Christ. Our problems started the day we got away from personal witnessing. Every preacher and layman, denominational servant and scholar, missionary and institutional representative should do the work of an evangelist.

You can't have doubts about the Bible and be a soulwinner at the same time. The evangelist can't evangelize if he has misgivings about his evangel. As you go into the homes of the lost, what you believe about the Bible is absolutely crucial.

Step with me into a modest home. The carpet is smelly; beer cans are scattered around; the family is holding together by a thread. We are looking into the face of a man whose eternal destiny is on the line. He is an alcoholic; his son is on drugs; his girl is pregnant. "Sir, let me share with you some verses from Romans. But we are not sure Paul wrote it. Maybe the disciples forged his name to lend credibility to their work. This book of Romans says, *all have sinned*. We are sinners because of the fall of Adam and Eve in Eden. But we aren't sure there was a garden of Eden or that Adam and Eve ever existed. It also says, *Christ died for our sins*. But don't make more of that than you should. He died to set an example for you to follow. He is reported to have said, *Come unto Me and I will give you rest*. Could I interest you in having an existential encounter with the spirit of Jesus which is alive in the universe somewhere?" The man replies, "No thanks, but if you have the phone numbers of AA, Drug Rehab, or Planned Parenthood, I would like them."

If you don't have a trustworthy Bible, you are out of business in the homes of lost people. Let's get on with our evangelical imperative. Let's fill the highways and byways with Baptists and their Bibles, sharing the good news with a lost world.

The Bible has:

C. ESCHATOLOGICAL Implications (4:6-13)

Paul's thoughts now turn eschatological to last things. Not prophetically, but personally. He is facing his own death. *I am ready to be offered* (poured out like a drink offering) ... *the time for my departure* (loosing of tent cords) *is at hand*. What did Paul want in the last days? Verse 13 tells us. He wanted his "cloak," something warm for his body; his "books," something stimulating for his mind; but "especially the parchments." He wanted the Word of God for his soul.

I wonder what Old Testament portions he wanted as soft pillows on his deathbed? Was it Job 19:25-26, *For I know that my Redeemer liveth, and that He shall stand at the latter day upon the earth; and though after my skin, worms destroy this body, yet in my flesh shall I see God*? Or was it Psalm 23:4, *Yea, though I walk through the valley of the shadow of death, I will fear no evil; for Thou art with me; Thy rod and Thy staff, they comfort me*?

I don't especially like funerals; but, like all preachers, I don't refuse to conduct them. When I stand before a broken-hearted family I need something to bring them comfort. I have a Book! I have never seen it fail. I have seen the Word of God brush tears from eyes and pour the balm of Gilead on hurting hearts. Romans 15:4 says, *Whatsoever things were written beforetime were written for our learning, that we through patience and comfort of the Scriptures might have hope.*

If you have no trustworthy Bible, you have nothing to give hope to those who are facing death. A pastor sowed seeds of doubt about the Bible in the minds of his congregation. A critically ill member sent for him. "Shall I read from the Bible and pray with you?" "Yes," said the dying man. His wife brought his Bible. As the pastor opened it, he found certain books missing. Some chapters were gone, verses were cut out. It was a shamefully mutilated Bible. The startled pastor exclaimed, "Have you not a better Bible than this one?" Accusingly the dying man said, "When you came to our church, I had a whole Bible. You told us certain books were fictional, and I cut them out. You told us some chapters were not true, and I removed them. You said certain verses were not accurate, so I cut them out, too. There is little of my Bible left except the two covers." When you come to die, what kind of Bible do you want? Look to your left—see the deathbeds of those who die denying any part of the Bible. Show me the triumphant death of one who rejected the Scriptures. There are no smiles of hope, no shouts of joy, only darkness and despair and doubt. Now, look to the right—see the deathbeds of those with the whole Bible in their hands. See the radiance on their faces. Listen to the shouts of victory!

> There is just one Book for the dying,
>
> One Book for the starting tears,
>
> And one for the soul that is going home,
>
> For the numberless years.
>
> There is just one Book.

Years ago, in the days of the old Camp Meetings, a preacher set out after the evening service to find his way along the edge of a dangerous cliff to the cottage where he was to spend the night. He had no lantern; flashlights were then unknown. An old farmer, sensing the preacher's predicament lighted a bundle of pine branches, handed them to the preacher saying, "Take this, it will light your way home." The preacher said, "But what if the wind blows it out?" "It will see you home." "But, what if the rain extinguishes it?" "It will see you home." "But what if it burns out before I get there?" "It will see you home."

Do you see this Book? It is a lamp unto your feet and a light to your path. There will be times when winds of unbelief may seem to almost put out its glow. Storms of skepticism may threaten to engulf it. There may even be times when you are tempted to lay it aside and make your way unaided. At times it may look old-fashioned alongside the psychedelic flashlights of this age. But, my Baptist brothers and sisters, hold on to your Bible. It will see you home!

A Collection of Essays on Biblical Preaching in Honor of Jerry Vines

End Notes

A Brief Look into the Life of the Preacher: Jerry Vines by Emir and Ergun Caner

1   Jerry Vines, "A Baptist and His Bible" (Woodstock, Georgia: It's a New Day Ministries, Inc.), n.d.

2   Ibid.

3   Ibid.

4   Nancy Smith, "A Faithful Soldier," in *A Faithful Soldier*, eds. Nancy Smith and Stan Bethea (Jacksonville, FL: n.p., 2005), 12.

5   Emir and Ergun Caner, *The Sacred Trust: Sketches of the Southern Baptist Convention Presidents* (Nashville: Broadman and Holman, 2003), 177.

6   Smith, 13.

7   Later Vines recollects that he struggled with doubting his salvation, until, "while praying one afternoon by his bed, the Holy Spirit assured him that he was indeed saved." See Jeffrey Donovan Pennington, *The Preaching and Pastoral Ministry of Charles Jerry Vines: A Model of Evangelistic Focus* (Ph.D. diss., Southern Baptist Theological Seminary, 2011), 20.

8   Caner and Caner, 177.

9   Smith, 14.

10   Ibid.

11   Ibid. Vines states, "I think that's the bottom line, to encourage others to know Christ as their Savior" (15).

12   Pennington, 22.

13   Ibid., 23.

14   For more information about this liberal approach to Christianity, see Rudolf Bultmann, *Interpreting Faith for the Modern Era* (Minneapolis, MN: Fortress, Press), 1991.

15   During his sermon, "A Baptist and His Bible", Vines, reflecting upon this liberal theory of exegesis, asserted, "I'd rather heard

Balaam's donkey talk than some modernistic preachers preach."

16   Smith, 16.

17   Smith, 16-17.

18   Ibid., 18.

19   Ibid.

20   Caner and Caner, 178-79

21   Pennington, 33..

22   Smith, 19-20.

23   Pennington, 36-37.

24   Ibid., 37.

25   Ibid., 38-39.

26   Ibid., 39-40.

27   Ibid., 41.

28   Ibid., 41-42.

29   Caner and Caner, 179. The combined volume was entitled *Power in the Pulpit* which was edited by Jerry Vines and Jim Shaddix (Moody, 1999).

30   For a journalistic look into the Conservative Resurgence, see James Hefley, *The Conservative Resurgence in the Southern Baptist Convention* (Hannibal, MO: Hannibal Books, 1991).

31   For a personal memoir about the Conservative Resurgence, see Paul Pressler, *A Hill on Which to Die* (Nashville: B&H, 1999).

32   Carl L. Kell and L. Raymond Camp, *In the Name of the Father: The Rhetoric of the New Southern Baptist Covnention* (Carbondale, IL: SIU Press, 1999). In this work, by two authors admittedly unsympathetic to the conservative movement, they compare Vines to the Apostle Paul and call his sermon, "A Baptist and His Bible," the defining moment of the movement (56-57).

33   Caner and Caner, 179-180.

34 Pennington, 54.

35 With men like Dr. Vines, who holds to the view that Christ died for every person, on the Baptist Faith and Message committee, the revised confession is recognized by those on the committee as a broad document that does not view Scripture from a strictly Reformed paradigm.

36 Smith, 25-26; Pennington, 55-57.

37 For varying press coverage about his statements and their veracity, see Norm Miller and Joni Hannigan, "Comments about Muhammad Originate in Key Islamic Source" (Baptist Press; 13 June 2002), at http://www.bpnews.net/bpnews.asp?id=13602 and "Muslims Angered by Baptist Criticism (CNN, 13 June 2002), at http://edition.cnn.com/2002/ALLPOLITICS/06/13/cf.crossfire/; accessed 6 August 2012.

38 Art Toalston, "Jerry Vines To Stay On The Go After 23-Year FL Pastorate" (Baptist Press, 12 May 2005), http://www.bpnews.net/bpnews.asp?id=20778; accessed 6 August 2012.

Simple Biblicism: The Word of God in the Theology of Jerry Vines by Malcolm B. Yarnell III

1 Jerry Vines, "A Baptist and His Bible" (unpublished manuscript), ll.

2 Adrian Rogers, Foreword to Vines, "A Baptist and His Bible."

3 Most compactly, though not exhaustively, in Malcolm B. Yarnell III, *The Formation of Christian Doctrine* (Nashville: B&H Academic, 2007).

4 I have treated this problem elsewhere. Yarnell, "Why Am I a Biblicist?" (SBC Today, July 2011) available at http://sbctoday.com/2011/07/28/why-am-i-a-biblicist/.

5 Vines, Sermon on Luke 24: 13-19, 25-27, 31-35 (unpublished manuscript).

6 Neo-orthodoxy was originally a movement away from liberalism, significantly in the biography of its leading pastor-theologian, Karl Barth. Eberhard Busch, *Karl Barth: His Life from Letters and Autobiographical Texts*, transl. John Bowden (Philadelphia: Fortress Press, 1976).

7   E.g. Vines, Sermon on John 1:1-5, 14, 18 (unpublished manuscript).

8   "Your whole Bible is a hymn book that points to Jesus. ... It is Jesus, Jesus, Jesus all the way through the Bible." Vines, Sermon on Luke 24:13-19, 25-27, 31-35. On Divine love, see below.

9   Vines, "Sermon on John 3:16," in *Whosoever Will: A Biblical-Theological Critique of Five-Point Calvinism: Reflections from the John 3:16 Conference*, ed. by David L. Allen and Steve W. Lemke (Nashville: B&H Academic, 2010), 14.

10 Vines, Sermon on Hebrews 4:12-13 (unpublished manuscript).

11 Vines, "A Baptist and His Bible," Preface.

12 Vines, "A Baptist and His Bible," I.

13 Cf. "The Bible is like a divine kaleidoscope. Every turn reveals new beauty and wonder. So variegated is the word of God that no one definition is sufficient to explain it. So multi-faceted is the Bible that no one description is adequate to display it." Vines, Sermon on Hebrews 4:12-13.

14 For more on this theological error, see Yarnell, "Whose Jesus? Which Revelation?" *Midwestern Journal of Theology*, 1.1-2 (Spring 2003): 33-53.

15 Vines, "A Baptist and His Bible," II.

16 Vines, Sermon on John 1:1-5, 14, 18.

17 Vines, "Stargazers or Soul-Winners? 'This Same Jesus Shall So Come," in *The Return of Christ: A Premillennial Perspective: Reflections from the Acts 1:11 Conference*, ed. David L. Allen and Steve W. Lemke (Nashville: B&H Academic, 2011), 14-15.

18 Ibid., 16.

19 Ibid., 10-11.

20 Vines, Sermon on Romans 10, in *By the Book: A Chapter by Chapter Bible Study Series from Jerry Vines Ministries* (Jerry Vines Ministries, 2008).

21 Vines, "Sermon on John 3:16," 17.

22	This claim for the priority of Divine love is in stark contrast to John Piper's claim for the priority of Divine glory. Piper's imbalanced doctrine of God is the basis for his antinomian-tinged doctrine of "Christian hedonism." Even Piper's own church seems to have intuited this imbalance. Piper's response, while citing Divine love, dwells upon Divine holiness instead. John Piper, *Brothers, We Are Not Professionals: A Plea to Pastors for Radical Ministry* (Nashville: Broadman & Holman, 2002), 5-16. Vines's argument for the priority of Divine love corrects such imbalances. Vines, "Sermon on John 3:16," 16.
23	Vines, Sermon on John 17:6-9 (unpublished manuscript).
24	Vines, "Sermon on John 3:16," 26.
25	Ibid., 27.
26	Ibid., 25.
27	Vines, Sermon on John 1:1-5, 14, 18.
28	Vines, Sermon on Hebrews 4:12-13.
29	Vines, Sermon on Luke 24:13-19, 25-27, 31-35. Dr. Vines noted he had preached some ten sermons on this same text.
30	Vines, Sermon on John 17:6-19.
31	Vines, Sermon on Romans 10.

The Preaching Event: A True Baptist Distinctive by O.S. Hawkins

1	Baptist Press, Nashville, Tennessee, May 13, 1996 (Article entitled – *Altar Calls: Appropriate for Appealing to the Lost?*)
2	Charles Grandison Finney, *Lectures on Revival of Religion* (New York: Revell, 1835, 1968 reprint), 223.

The Church's Necessity for 21st Century Survival by Steven Smith

1	*The Holy Bible: English Standard Version.* 2001 (Titus 1:9). Wheaton: Standard Bible Society.
2	See "*A Strange Friendship*", Chapter 12 in Harry Stout's Divine Dramatist. Grand Rapids: Eerdmans, 1991.

3   Luke 15:1-32

4   John 4:1-30

5   John 8:1-10

6   Luke 19:1-10

7   *The Holy Bible: English Standard Version*. 2001 (2 Timothy 3:14–17). Wheaton: Standard Bible Society.

8   Luke 24:27; 44-49

Preaching the Whole Counsel of God by Paige Patterson

1   W. A. Criswell, "The Pastor in the Pulpit," in Criswell's Guidebook for Pastors (Nashville: Broadman Press, 1980), 41-42.

2   All citations from Jerry Vines except those with a book reference were secured in an interview with Dr. Vines on March 15, 2012.

3   Charles W. Koller, "The Scriptural Conception of Preaching," in Expository Preaching without Notes (Grand Rapids: Baker Book House, 1969), 15.

4   Eric W. Hayden, introduction to Preaching Through the Bible (Grand Rapids: Zondervan Publishing House, 1964), n.p.

5   Ibid.

6   Jeff D. Ray, "The Advantages of Expository Preaching," in Expository Preaching (Grand Rapids: Zondervan, 1940), 55.

7   Clarence E. Macartney, "The Recall to Gospel Preaching," in Preaching without Notes (New York and Nashville: Abingdon Press, 1976), 9-10.

8   Jerry Vines and Jim Shaddix, "Defining the Task," in Power in the Pulpit: How to Prepare and Deliver Expository Sermons (Chicago: Moody Press, 1999), 33.

9   Criswell, Criswell's Guidebook for Pastors, 61.

A Collection of Essays on Biblical Preaching in Honor of Jerry Vines

Measuring Success in Biblical Preaching by Stephen Rummage

1. Throughout this chapter, I will be relying on *A Practical Guide to Sermon Preparation* (Chicago: Moody Press, 1985) and *A Guide to Effective Sermon Delivery* (Chicago: Moody Press, 1986), as my primary sources. I do this with full recognition of and great appreciation for Dr. Vines's later work, *Power in the Pulpit: How to Prepare and Deliver Expository Sermons* (Chicago: Moody Press, 1999), which he wrote in collaboration with my colleague and friend Jim Shaddix. I have chosen to focus on the earlier books because (1) they were so highly influential in my own formation as a preacher and (2) they represent exclusively Dr. Vines's own approach to preaching.

2. Vines, *A Practical Guide to Sermon Preparation*, xii.

3. Ibid., 4.

4. Ibid., 6-7. Dr. Vines's description is reminiscent of an influential expanded definition of expository preaching offered by Faris Whitesell in *Power in Expository Preaching* (Old Tappan, NJ: Revell, 1963), xi.

5. Ibid., 7-8.

6. Ibid., 19.

7. Ibid., 111.

8. Ibid., 112.

9. Who is in his right mind would contribute to a volume honoring Jerry Vines and come out against alliterated outlines? I find Dr. Vines's frequent use of alliteration effective, efficient, and edifying! Plus, I regularly use alliteration myself. I'm just saying, sometimes sermonizers should shun sentences starting with same-sounding syllables.

10. Vines, *A Practical Guide to Sermon Preparation*, 6.

11. Ibid., 4.

12. Vines, *A Guide to Effective Sermon Delivery*, 148

13. Ibid., 150.

14. Vines, *A Practical Guide to Sermon Preparation*, 70.

15   Ibid., 160.

16   Vines, *A Practical Guide to Sermon Preparation*, 10.

17   Ibid., 170.

A Theology of Expository Preaching by Steve Lemke

1   Jerry Vines, *A Baptist and His Bible* (Jacksonville, FL: First Baptist Church of Jacksonville, 1987), 1.

2   Jerry Vines and Jim Shaddix, *Power in the Pulpit: How to Prepare and Deliver Expository Sermons* (Chicago: Moody Press, 1999), 28.

3   Ibid., 27.

4   Ibid., 28.

5   For examples of Dr. Vines' expositions, see Jerry Vines, *A Journey through the Bible: From Genesis to Malachi* (Carrollton, GA: Free Church Press, 2011); Jerry Vines, *A Journey through the Bible: From Matthew to Revelation* (Carrollton, GA: Free Church Press, 2011); Jerry Vines, *Basic Bible Sermons from the Ten Commandments* (Nashville: Broadman, 1992); Jerry Vines, *God's Perfect 10: Studies from Exodus 20* (N.p., Jerry Vines, 2006); Jerry Vines, *Pursuing God's Own Heart: Lessons from the Life of David* (Nashville: Broadman and Holman, 2003); Jerry Vines, *Immortal Kombat: A Study of the Book of Job* (N.p., Jerry Vines, 2007); Jerry Vines and John Phillips, *Exploring the Book of Daniel* (Neptune, NJ: Loizeaux Brothers, 1990); Jerry Vines, *Exploring the Gospels: Mark* (Neptune, NJ: Loizeaux Brothers, 1990); Jerry Vines, *Acts Alive: A Witnessing Church in the 21st Century* (Jacksonville, FL: First Baptist Church of Jacksonville, 2007); Jerry Vines, *God Speaks Today: A Study of 1 Corinthians* (Grand Rapids: Zondervan, 1979); Jerry Vines, *The Corinthian Confusion: A Study of 1 Corinthians* (N.p., Jerry Vines, 2005); Jerry Vines, *The Believer's Guide to Hebrews* (Neptune, NJ: Loizeaux Brothers, 1993); Jerry Vines, *Exploring 1, 2, 3 John* (Neptune, NJ: Loizeaux Brothers, 1989); and Jerry Vines, *Acts Alive: A Witnessing Church in the 21st Century* (Jacksonville, FL: First Baptist Church of Jacksonville, 2007).

6   For an eyewitness account of this battle, see "Out of the Stands, Onto the Sideline, and Into the Game," a Convocation address by Charles S. Kelley Jr. at New Orleans Baptist Theological Seminary on September 7, 2000. Available online in the Resources section of the Baptist Center for Theology and Ministry website at http://www.baptistcenter.com/resources/Essays%20and%20White%20Papers/Archived%20Papers/Kelley%20-%20Essay%20on%20BFM%20Article%20One.pdf.

7   This is a variation of a statement attributed to George Santayana in *The Life of Reason* (New York: Prometheus, 1998), 82. Winston Churchill and many others have repeated variations of this proverbial saying.

8   G. K. Chesterton, *Orthodoxy* (New York: John Lane, 1908), 212.

9   Danny Akin, "Southern Baptists: There Is a Future if ..." presentation at "The Mission of Today's Church," the annual conference of the Baptist Center for Theology and Ministry, on February 11, 2005.

10   William H. Willimon, "Been There, Preached That: Today's Conservatives Sound Like Yesterday's Liberals," *Leadership* 16 (Fall 1995):76-77.

11   Ibid., 78.

12   Francis A. Schaeffer, *He Is There and He Is Not Silent* (Wheaton: Tyndale House, 1972); Carl F. H. Henry, *God, Revelation, and Authority: God Who Speaks and Shows*, 6 vols. (Waco, Word: 1976-1983).

13   Article II of the *Baptist Faith and Message 2000* twice describes God as "all powerful" and "all knowing," and adds that "His perfect knowledge extends to all things, past, present, and future, including the future decisions of His free creatures." It also describes God as "all wise" and "all loving," "infinite in holiness and all other perfections." Dr. Vines was a member of the committee that framed the *Baptist Faith and Message 2000* statement, the doctrinal confession of the Southern Baptist Convention.

14   The *Baptist Faith and Message 2000*, Article II.

15   The *Baptist Faith and Message 2000* affirms not only that God the Father is "all loving," but also that "He is fatherly in His attitude toward all men." *Baptist Faith and Message 2000*, Article 2A: "God the Father."

16   See the sermon by Jerry Vines on John 3:16 for the John 3:16 Conference sponsored by Jerry Vines Ministries, in Jerry Vines, "Sermon on John 3:16," in *Whosoever Will: A Biblical-Theological Critique of Five Point Calvinism. Reflections on the John 3:16 Conference*, ed. David Allen and Steve Lemke (Nashville: B&H Academic, 2010), 13-28.

17   For a glimpse of Dr. Vine's Christology, see Jerry Vines, *Great Events in the Life of Christ* (Wheaton: Victor Books, 1979); and Jerry Vines, *Interviews with Jesus* (Nashville: Broadman, 1981).

18   *The Baptist Faith and Message 2000*, Article I, "The Scriptures."

19   C. H. Dodd, *The Apostolic Preaching and Its Developments* (New York: Harper and Row, 1964), 7-35.

20   Dr. Vines' Pneumatology is outlined in Jerry Vines, *SpiritLife: Experience the Power, Excitement, and Intimacy of God's Shaping Hand* (Nashville: Broadman and Holman, 1998); Jerry Vines, *SpiritWorks: Charismatic Practices and the Bible* (Nashville: Broadman and Holman, 1999); and Jerry Vines, *SpiritFruit: The Graces of the Spirit-Filled Life* (Nashville: Broadman and Holman, 2000). These three books have been combined into Jerry Vines, *The Spirit Book* (Collierville, TN: Innovo Publishing, 2010).

21   Vines and Shaddix, 27.

22   Some describe the Spirit's work in leading a person to salvation as the "solicitous call," as "prevenient grace," or as "enabling grace." See Richard Land, "Congruent Election: Understanding Salvation from an 'Eternal Now' Perspective," in *Whosoever Will*, ed. Allen and Lemke, p. 59.

23   *The Baptist Faith and Message 2000*, Article 2C, "The Holy Spirit."

24   This is the position affirmed in the *Baptist Faith and Message 2000* (Article VI), and in every major Baptist confession in church history (including not only the *Baptist Faith and Message* of 1925, 1963, and 2000, but also in Calvinistic Baptist affirmations such as the *Second London Confession*

and the *Philadelphia Confession*. For a scriptural defense of pastor/teachers, elders, and bishops being the same office, see Steve Lemke, "The Elder in the Early Church," *Biblical Illustrator* 19 (Fall 1992): 59-62; Gerald Cowen, *Who Rules the Church? Examining Congregational Leadership and Church Government*, with a foreword by Jerry Vines and appendices by Emir E. Caner and Stephen Prescott (Nashville: Broadman and Holman, 2003); and Gerald Cowan, "An Elder and His Ministry: From a Baptist Perspective," *Journal for Baptist Theology and Ministry* 3, no. 1 (Spring 2005): 56-73.

The Importance of Biblical Preaching in Building a Great Church by Adam B. Dooley

1 See Jerry Vines and Jim Shaddix, *Power in the Pulpit* (Chicago: Moody Press, 1999), 33. Despite his latter commitment to Bible exposition, Vines readily confesses he was a topical preacher before his exposure to the teaching of Warren Wiersbe.

2 Daniel Akin, "A Crisis in the 21st Century Preaching: A Mandate for Biblical Exposition," (danielakin.com), accessed May 24, 2012.

3 All Scripture references are taken from the *New American Standard Bible*, The Lockman Foundation, 1995.

Biblical Preaching in a Mega-Church Setting by Mac Brunson

1 Bruce Catton, *Mr. Lincoln's Army* (Garden City, N.Y.: Doubleday, 1951), 29, 34.

2 Martin Lloyd-Jones, *Preaching and Preachers* (London: Hodder and Stoughton, 1971).

3 Dietrich Bonhoeffer, *The Cost of Discipleship* (London: SCM Press, 1962), p. 7.

4 Eric C. Malte, "Preaching from the Greek New Testament," *Concordia Theological Monthly* 25 (September 1954): 656.

Do the Work of an Evangelist by Jeff Pennington

1. Carl L. Kell and L. Raymond Camp, *In the Name of the Father: The Rhetoric of the New Southern Baptist Convention* (Carbondale: Southern Illinois University Press, 1999), 56.

2. Jerry Vines, email interview by author, 7 June 2010.

3. Jeffrey D. Pennington, "The Preaching and Pastoral Ministry of Charles Jerry Vines: A Model of Evangelistic Focus" (Ph.D. diss., The Southern Baptist Theological Seminary, 2011), 4.

4. Ibid., 35-36. Timothy Hight made a similar observation in Timothy A. Hight, "A Comparative Homiletical Analysis of Selected Southern Baptist Convention Presidents from 1979 through 1989" (Th.D. diss., Mid-America Baptist Theological Seminary, 1991), 36.

5. Jerry Vines, *A Practical Guide to Sermon Preparation* (Chicago: Moody, 1985), 53.

6. Jerry Vines, "The Church's Main Business," An audio recorded message of an exposition of Matthew 28:16-20 delivered at First Baptist Church, Jacksonville, FL, 2003; CD. In this message, Vines explains this quote as "the irresistible logic of the church." In a personal interview with the author 25 August 2009, he refers to this concept as the "irresistible logic of the Bible" and the "irresistible logic of evangelism."

7. Calvin Carr, personal interview by author, 14 April 2010.

8. Hayes Wicker, O. S. Hawkins, and Nelson Sturgill, "Church Members, SBC Leaders Reflect on Vines' Ministry," *Florida Baptist Witness*, 16 February 2006 [on-line]; accessed 19 October 2006; available from http://www.floridabaptistwitness.com/ 5505.article; Internet.

9. Jerry Vines, personal interview by author, 17 August 2006. When Vines speaks of a church's "soul-consciousness," he speaks of a congregation's corporate embrace of the irresistible logic of the Bible.

10. Vines, *A Practical Guide*, 30.

11. Jerry Vines, personal interview by author, 25 August 2009.

12. Emir Caner and Ergun Caner, *The Sacred Trust: Sketches of the Southern Baptist Convention Presidents* (Nashville:

Broadman and Holman, 2003), 178.

13 Nancy Smith, "A Faithful Soldier," in *A Faithful Soldier*, ed. Nancy Smith and Stan Bethea (Jacksonville, FL: n.p., 2005), 19.

14 Statistics obtained in email to author 18 October 2006 from Kathleen Harris, Research Services, Georgia Baptist Convention.

15 Statistics obtained in email to author, 13 October 2006 from Mickey W. Crawford, Statistical Programmer, Alabama Baptist State Board of Missions.

16 Statistics obtained on 11 October 2006 from Rachel D. Tracey, Department Secretary for Information Support Services, Florida Baptist Convention.

17 Timothy A. Hight, "A Comparative Homiletical Analysis of Selected Southern Baptist Convention Presidents from 1979 through 1989" (Th.D. diss., Mid-America Baptist Theological Seminary, 1991), 39-40.

18 Homar G. Lindsay Jr. and Jerry Vines, *The Miracle of Downtown Jacksonville* (Jacksonville, FL: n.p.), SS-2-SS-6.

19 Jerry Vines to Landrum Leavell, letter, 12 July 1988, Jerry Vines Papers, Southern Baptist Historical Library and Archives, Nashville.

20 Janet Vines, a personal interview by author, 25 August 2009.

21 Jerry Vines, a personal interview with author, 17 August 2006.

22 Jerry Vines, *Acts Alive: A Witnessing Church in the Twenty-First Century* (Atlanta, GA: n.p., 2007).

23 Ibid., 5.

24 The term "continuous lifestyle evangelism," comes from Jerry Vines, "Evangelistic Preaching and the Book of Acts," *Criswell Theological Review* 5.1 (1990): 83. I prefer Vines' term "continuous lifestyle evangelism" over the term he uses in his later works, "lifestyle evangelism." His earlier term is better at conveying his approach to personal evangelism. It highlights the continuous aspect of a person's witness and also serves to slightly distinguish his approach from that of Joe Aldrich.

25 Joe Aldrich, *Lifestyle Evangelism: Learning to Open Your Life to Those Around You* (Sisters, OR: Multnomah, 1993), 5-6.

26 Vines, *Acts Alive*, 9

27 Vines, *Witnesses Alive*, 6.

28 Ibid., 7.

29 Vines, *Acts Alive*, 9.

30 Vines, *Witnesses Alive*, 11.

31 Ibid., 12.

32 Ibid., 12-13.

33 Vines, *Witnesses Alive*, 27.

34 Vines, *Acts Alive*, 31.

35 Ibid.

36 Ibid., 32.

37 Ibid., 41.

38 Ibid., 50.

39 Ibid., 48.

40 Jerry Vines and Jim Shaddix, *Power in the Pulpit: How to Prepare and Deliver Expository Sermon* (Chicago: Moody Press, 1999), 218.

41 Vines, *A Practical Guide*, 146.

42 Jerry Vines, email correspondence by author, 24 October 2008.

43 Jerry Vines, "A World in a Week" [on-line]; a sermon manuscript of an exposition of Genesis 1:3-31 delivered at First Baptist church, Jacksonville, FL; accessed 27 March 2008; available from http://www.sermonsearch.com; Internet.

44 For a survey of the evangelistic twist and insights into principles of the twist and pitfalls for an expositor to avoid, see Pennington, "The Preaching and Pastoral Ministry of Charles Jerry Vines," 132-146.

45	Thom S. Rainer, "A Resurgence Not Yet Realized: Evangelistic Effectiveness in the Southern Baptist Convention Since 1979," *Southern Baptist Journal of Theology* 9.1 (2005): 55.
46	Ibid., 54-69. Since this article was published, the convention's annual baptism numbers have not improved. See Art Toalston, "Impact of 'Everyone Can' assessed," *Baptist Press* (17 April 2007), [on-line]; accessed on 12 March 2009; available from http://www.sbcbaptistpress.org/BPnews.asp?ID=25409; Internet.

Growing a Church through Evangelistic, Biblical Preaching by Steve Gaines

1	Quote attributed to both G. Campbell Morgan and Stuart Holden in Stott, *Between Two Worlds*, 294.
2	Roy Fish, "Church Evangelism" (Class notes, Southwestern Baptist Theological Seminary, 1981).
3	Phillips Brooks, *Lectures on Preaching* (New York: E. P. Dutton and Company, 1880), 5.
4	W. A. Criswell, *Criswell's Guidebook for Pastors* (Nashville: Broadman Press, 1980), 54.
5	C. H. Spurgeon, *The Soul-Winner: How to Lead Sinners to the Saviour* (Grand Rapids: Wm. B. Eerdmans Publishing Company, 1963),106-107.
6	Richard Stoll Armstrong, *The Pastor as Evangelist* (Philadelphia: The Westminster Press, 1984), 21.
7	Cp. John 16:8.
8	Cp. Titus 3:5.
9	Lloyd Perry, "Preaching with Power and with Purpose," *Christianity Today* 23 (Feb. 1979): 23.
10	Roy H. Short, *Evangelistic Preaching* (Nashville: Tidings, 1946), 14-16.
11	Lloyd Perry, *A Manuel for Biblical Preaching* (Grand Rapids: Baker Book House, 1965), 2.

12   Arthur T. Pierson, *Evangelistic Work* (London: Passmore and Alabaster, 1892), 12.

13   Lloyd M. Perry and John R. Strubhar, *Evangelistic Preaching*, (Eugene, Oregon: 2000). Section III, entitled "Selecting Material for Evangelistic Preaching" is most helpful.

14   Quoted in Lewis Drummond, *Spurgeon: Prince of Preachers* (Grand Rapids: Kregel Publications, 1992), 295.

15   Haddon W. Robinson, *Biblical Preaching: The Development and Delivery of Expository Messages* (Grand Rapids: Baker Book House, 1980), 20.

16   John R. Bisagno, *Letters to Timothy: A Handbook for Pastors* (Nashville: Broadman and Holman Publishers, 2001), 159.

17   Cp. Ezekiel 3:17-19.

18   Roy Fish, *Giving a Good Invitation* (Broadman Press: 1974).

19   O. S. Hawkins, *Drawing the Net* (Nashville: Broadman Press, 1993).

20   R. Alan Streett, *The Effective Invitation: A Practical Guide for Pastor's* (Grand Rapids: Kregel Publications, 1995).

21   Faris D. Whitesell, *65 Ways to Give Evangelistic Invitations* (Grand Rapids: Zondervan Publishing House, 1945).

22   Cp. Revelation 22:17.

23   1 Corinthians 1:17, NASB.

24   S. F. Olford, "The Power of Preaching," *Christianity Today* 23 (Dec. 1979): 22.

25   W. E. Sangster, *The Craft of Sermon Construction* (Grand Rapids, Michigan: Baker Book House, 1981), 24.

26   Cp. Ephesians 4:15.

A Collection of Essays on Biblical Preaching in Honor of Jerry Vines

Contributors

David L. Allen is presently Dean, School of Theology and Professor of Preaching Southwestern Baptist Theological Seminary in Fort Worth, TX. Dr. Allen received a Ph.D. from the University of Texas at Arlington.

Mac Brunson is Senior Pastor of the First Baptist Church, Jacksonville, FL. Dr. Brunson received a D.Min. from Southwestern Baptist Theological Seminary in Fort Worth, TX.

Emir Caner is President of Truett-McConnell College in Cleveland, GA. Dr. Caner received his Ph.D. in History from the University of Texas at Arlington.

Ergun Caner is Provost and Vice President for Academic Affairs at Arlington Baptist College, Arlington, TX. Dr. Caner received a D.Theol. from the University of South Africa.

Adam B. Dooley is Senior Pastor of the Dauphin Way Baptist Church in Mobile, AL. Dr. Dooley received a Ph.D. in Christian Preaching, Theology, and Evangelism from Southern Baptist Theological Seminary in Louisville, KY.

Steve Gaines is Senior Pastor of the Bellevue Baptist Church in Cordova, TN. Dr. Gaines received a Ph.D. in Preaching from Southwestern Baptist Theological Seminary in Fort Worth, TX.

Johnny Hunt is Senior Pastor of Woodstock First Baptist Church, Woodstock, GA. Dr. Hunt received an M.Div. from Southeastern Baptist Theological Seminary, Wake Forest, NC. In addition, Dr. Hunt has also received several honorary doctorates over the years for his outstanding work in ministry.

O. S. Hawkins is President of GuideStone Financial Resources of the Southern Baptist Convention. Dr. Hawkins served as pastor of several Southern Baptist churches, including the historic First Baptist Church, Dallas, TX before becoming president of GuideStone. Dr. Hawkins received his D.Min. from Luther Rice Seminary.

Steve Lemke is Provost and Professor of Philosophy and Ethics at New Orleans Baptist Theological Seminary, New Orleans, LA. Dr. Lemke received a Ph.D. from Southwestern Baptist Theological Seminary in Fort Worth, TX.

Peter Lumpkins is presently a bi-vocational pastor, small Christian publisher, editor, and writer. In addition to serving as editor for a small group Bible study curriculum covering the entire New Testament, Lumpkins also is author of *Alcohol Today: Abstinence in an Age of Indulgence* (Garland: Hannibal Books, 2009). Lumpkins received a B.A. in Humanities with a Specialty in Religion and Philosophy from Thomas Edison State College, Trenton, NJ and a M.Div. from New Orleans Baptist Theological Seminary, New Orleans, LA. He also completed additional graduate studies in Bioethics at Trinity Graduate School, Trinity Evangelical Divinity School, Deerfield, IL.

Paige Patterson is President of Southwestern Baptist Theological Seminary in Fort Worth, TX. Dr. Patterson received his Th.D. from the New Orleans Baptist Theological Seminary in New Orleans, LA.

Jeff Pennington is Executive Pastor of Buck Run Baptist Church in Frankfort, KY. Dr. Pennington received a Ph.D. in Evangelism from Southern Baptist theological Seminary in Louisville, KY.

Stephen Rummage serves as Senior Pastor of Bell Shoals Baptist Church in Brandon, Fl. Dr. Rummage received a Ph.D. in Preaching from New Orleans Baptist Theological Seminary, New Orleans, LA.

Steven Smith is Dean of the College at Southwestern and Professor of Communication, Southwestern Baptist Theological Seminary, Fort Worth, TX. Dr. Smith earned a Ph.D. in Communication at Regent University, Virginia Beach, VA.

Malcolm B. Yarnell III is presently Professor of Systematic Theology and Director of the Center for Theological Research at Southwestern Baptist Theological Seminary Fort in Worth, TX. Dr. Yarnell received a DPhil from Oxford University, Oxford, England.

A Collection of Essays on Biblical Preaching in Honor of Jerry Vines

Dr. Jerry Vines

Dr. Jerry Vines is a native of Carrollton, Georgia. He was educated at Mercer University (B.A.), New Orleans Theological Seminary (B.D.), and Luther Rice Seminary (Th.D.).

He was elected President of the Alabama Pastors' Conference in 1976, President of the Southern Baptist Pastors' Conference for 1976 -1977. He also served two terms as President of the Southern Baptist Convention from 1988 - 1989.

Dr. Vines accepted the call to be pastor at First Baptist Church, Jacksonville, Florida, in July 1982 and retired from the pastorate in February of 2006.

Dr. Vines' interests include Alabama football. It's a year-round passion! He also enjoys spending his free time in the Smoky Mountains with his family, especially his grandchildren! While there, it is a tradition for him to frequent The Old Mill restaurant for breakfast in Pigeon Forge, Tennessee.

He and his wife, Janet, have four children: two daughters, Joy and Jodi, and two sons, Jim and Jon. He and Mrs. Vines also have seven grandchildren: Brittney, Ashlyn, Jay, Caroline, Catherine, Jack and Carson.

A Collection of Essays on Biblical Preaching in Honor of Jerry Vines

Other Books by Free Church Press

Urgent: Igniting a Passion for Jesus, by Joe Donahue; Foreword by Ergun Caner. A personal story that many teens find themselves in today.

Ancient Wine and the Bible: The Case for Abstinence, by David R. Brumbelow; Foreword by Paige Patterson. Detailed study of wine, Scripture, and reasons for abstinence.

Green Pastures of a Barren Land: finding contentment in life's desolate seasons by Candise Farmer. Candise offers biblical encouragement to those facing difficult moments in life

Born Guilty? a Southern Baptist View of Original Sin by Adam Harwood. Published as an exclusive series by Free Church Press, Dr. Harwood challenges the popular Calvinistic notion that God counts the human race guilty of Adam's sin. Instead he defends the biblical-theological notion embraced by The Baptist Faith and Message (2000)--the only confession of faith the Southern Baptist Convention endorses as a convention—which states that human beings "inherit a nature and an environment inclined toward sin" and only when they are "capable of moral action" do they "become transgressors" and fall "under condemnation."
(order from freechurchpress.com and amazon.com)

Books by Dr. Jerry Vines

A Journey Through the Bible: From Genesis to Malachi, by Jerry Vines. Volume I. Introduction, outline, and synopsis of each Old Testament book by one of America's leading expositors

A Journey Through the Bible: From Matthew to Revelation, by Jerry Vines. Volume II. Introduction, outline, and synopsis of each New Testament book.

All the Days: Daily Devotions for Busy Believers, by Jerry Vines. An inspiring devotion for each day of the week.
(order from jerryvines.com, freechurchpress.com, amazon.com)

Preach the Word!

Other Books of Note

Alcohol Today: Abstinence in an Age of Indulgence, by Peter Lumpkins; Foreword by Jerry Vines. Published by Hannibal Books, a devastating argument against the use of a mind-altering drug.

(order through alcoholtoday.com and amazon.com)

Whosoever Will: A Biblical-Theological Critique of Five-Point Calvinism edited by David L. Allen and Steve W. Lemke. Published by B&H Academic, this volume remains the definitive challenge to the neo-Calvinist Resurgence in evangelicalism generally and within the Southern Baptist Convention particularly.

(order from amazon.com and Lifeway Christian Resources)

Hebrews: an Exegetical and Theological Exposition of Holy Scripture by David. L. Allen. Part of the New American Commentary series published by B&H Academic, Dr. Allen's treatment represents the premier commentary on the Book of Hebrews.

(order from amazon.com and Lifeway Christian Resources)

The Formation of Christian Doctrine by Malcolm B. Yarnell III. Published by B&H Academic, Dr. Yarnell focuses on the development of biblical theology from a decidedly Free Church perspective.

(order from amazon.com and Lifeway Christian Resources)

Revelation: an Exegetical and Theological Exposition of Holy Scripture by Paige Patterson. Part of the New American Commentary series published by Holman Reference, Dr. Patterson's treatment represents the premier commentary on the Book of Revelation.

(order from amazon.com and Lifeway Christian Resources)

The Spiritual Condition of Infants: A Biblical-Historical Survey and Systematic Proposal by Adam Harwood. Published by Wipf & Stock Publishers, Dr. Harwood's challenge to the Reformed doctrine of Original Sin constitutes the best critique to date of one of Augustinianism's major planks of belief.

(order from Wipf & Stock Publishers and amazon.com)

www.ingramcontent.com/pod-product-compliance
Lightning Source LLC
Chambersburg PA
CBHW060512090426
42735CB00011B/2195